BFI FILM CLASSICS

THE BLUE ANGEL
(DER BLAUE ENGEL)

....

S. S. Prawer

bfi Publishing

First published in 2002 by the
BRITISH FILM INSTITUTE
21 Stephen Street, London W1T 1LN

The British Film Institute
promotes greater understanding
and appreciation of, and
access to, film and moving image
culture in the UK.

British Library Cataloguing-in-Publication Data
A catalogue record for this book is available from the British Library

ISBN 0–85170–935–4

Series design by
Andrew Barron & Collis Clements Associates

Typeset in Fournier and Franklin Gothic by
D R Bungay Associates, Burghfield, Berks

Printed in Great Britain by Cromwell Press, Trowbridge, Wiltshire

BFI FILM CLASSICS

. . . .

Rob White
SERIES EDITOR

Edward Buscombe, Colin MacCabe, David Meeker and Markku Salmi
SERIES CONSULTANTS

Launched in 1992, BFI Film Classics is a series of books that introduces, interprets and honours 360 landmark works of world cinema. The series includes a wide range of approaches and critical styles, reflecting the diverse ways we appreciate, analyse and enjoy great films.

A treasury that keeps on delivering ... any film person needs the whole collection.
Independent on Sunday

Magnificently concentrated examples of flowing freeform critical poetry.
Uncut

A formidable body of work collectively generating some fascinating insights into the evolution of cinema.
Times Higher Education Supplement

The definitive film companion essays.
Hotdog

The choice of authors is as judicious, eclectic and original as the choice of titles.
Positif

Estimable.
Boston Globe

Invaluable.
Los Angeles Times

We congratulate the BFI for responding to the need to restore an informed level of critical writing for the general cinephile.
Canadian Journal of Film Studies

Well written, impeccably researched and beautifully presented ... as a publishing venture, it is difficult to fault.
Film Ireland

Josef von Sternberg and Emil Jannings, photographed in Berlin

CONTENTS

· ·

To the memory of the late
ISSOR and ROSE AVNER
who offered hospitality and shelter
at a time of greatest need
this book is gratefully dedicated

ACKNOWLEDGMENTS

. . . .

I am grateful for help and encouragement to my friends H.-M. Bock, Helga Belach, Margaret Dériaz and Anton Kaes, to Gero Gandert and the librarians and staff of the Berlin Stiftung Deutsche Kinemathek (now Filmmuseum Berlin), and to the editor of the BFI Film Classics series, Rob White. Above all I am indebted to the authors of the books listed in the Select Bibliography, who have enriched my knowledge and understanding of Sternberg's work – especially Luise Discherl and Gunther Nickel, Werner Sudendorf, and Peter Baxter.

Sternberg edited the German language version of *Der Blaue Engel/The Blue Angel* himself, but left the final cut of the simultaneously shot English version to others. I shall briefly refer to the textual problems this opens in an Appendix, but will not consider it in the main body of the book, whose analyses are based on the German language version described by Eckhart Schmidt in '*Der blaue Engel*. Protokoll', pp. 47–60, now conveniently reprinted in Discherl and Nickel, *Der blaue Engel. Die Drehbuchentwürfe*, pp. 423–510, along with an indispensable 'Chronik zur Entstehung der Films' by Werner Sudendorf. I have also consulted, with profit, the authorised translation of the German continuity issued by Lorrimer Publishing in 1968, with an instructive introduction by Sternberg himself.

Of the two spellings of the German title – *Der Blaue Engel* and *Der blaue Engel* – I prefer the former because it suggests more clearly that it originally designated an inn-sign and not a supernatural being, a figure in a painting, or a particular filmstar. The conjunction of 'blau' and 'Engel' does, however, have cultural implications in their German context that will be discussed in the present book. Unless the context demands otherwise, I shall use the familiar English title '*The Blue Angel*' when discussing the German version which is my principal subject. *Italics* will indicate the title, while 'The Blue Angel' in roman will denote the dockside establishment in which Lola Lola performs. I shall also follow the convention, adopted by characters in the film as well as most commentators, of abbreviating that stage name to a simple 'Lola'.

PROLOGUE

One need not have seen the film to recognise the image: a scantily dressed woman, in a costume that reveals a generous amount of bare thigh set off by black suspenders, sitting on a beer barrel clasping an upraised knee with both hands while she leans slightly back. This icon has featured, as a quotation, in many diverse films: Visconti's *La caduta degli dei* (*The Damned*), Cavani's *Il portiere di notte* (*The Night Porter*), Bergman's *The Serpent's Egg* and Fosse's *Cabaret*, in all of which *The Blue Angel* is

Cabaret (above left), *Shanghai Express* (above right); cartoon by Michael Heath reproduced with permission from The Spectator (1828) Ltd.

associated with Nazism and also with sado-masochism and/or homosexuality. Fassbinder played characteristic variations on its plot in *Lola*. The eponymous cabaret dancer of Deray's *Lola* has the same name, and a similar profession, as Sternberg's protagonist, though the film itself owes more to Ophüls than to Sternberg. Blakemore's *Privates on Parade* plays some of the familiar imagery for laughs; Madonna and Nicole Kidman have worn imitations of some of its costumes, as has Katja Flint in Vilsmaier's *Marlene*. Political cartoonists have superimposed others' heads on Dietrich's body: Heinrich Mann's in *Die Brennessel* (4 January 1933), Margaret Thatcher's in *The Spectator* (19 June 1993). There was a forgettable Hollywood remake in 1959, and stage adaptations have been seen in various countries, none of which, however, enjoyed long runs. The songs featured in it were an instant popular success, aided by gramophone and radio; Dietrich herself repeated them many times in cabaret performances, and others – notably Ute Lemper – followed suit. Deray's *Borsalino* introduces a chorus line of six girls being rehearsed in a cabaret called 'L'Ange bleu', and there has been a pop group that called itself 'Die blauen Engel'. Central performances in Dietrich's later films – Amy Jolly in *Morocco*, Shanghai Lily in *Shanghai Express*, Frenchy in *Destry Rides Again*, Erika in *A Foreign Affair* – all owe something to the Lola whom she so fascinatingly impersonated. *The Blue Angel* did for the German sound film what René Clair's *Sous les Toits de Paris* did for French and Hitchcock's *Blackmail* for English films: it showed up for the first time the full artistic possibilities opened up when films learned to talk, sing, play music and select from the manifold noises of the world in which we live those which affect, or reflect, mood and accompany significant actions. It also showed up the valuable effects that can be gained by the cessation of sound, the achievement of silence. It precipitated a German actress onto the world stage, and made her an indelible icon. It is a considerable work of art, marking an important stage in the work of a highly original director and in the history of the German cinema. It fully deserves its place in a series devoted to Film Classics.

1

. . . .

WHY IS THE ANGEL BLUE?

The German language version of *The Blue Angel* premièred on 1 April 1930, under the title *Der Blaue Engel*, in Berlin's luxurious and capacious Gloria-Palast cinema. It was not Germany's first sound film – but it was the most prestigious so far. The commissioning studio (UFA, Universum Film Aktiengesellschaft) had grown out of an organisation founded during World War I by the German government and army to counter enemy propaganda, and had recently come under the control of a staunchly right-wing press baron and a group of industrialists and bankers whose chief business manager, Ludwig Klitzsch, was given the task of finding a project that would unite cultural prestige with the kind of popularity that promised commercial success. This was to inaugurate UFA's newly built sound stages: a cruciform arrangement of four studios with built-in sound equipment grouped around a central administrative area. Intricate negotiations had been necessary to obtain workable patents, some in German, some in foreign hands; these were ultimately united in Klangfilm, which installed recording equipment and came to a mutually beneficial agreement with Tobis, which fitted sound projectors into cinemas. Klitzsch lured back Erich Pommer, a successful producer who had found new fields for his energies and enterprise in the USA, to head a production company within the UFA organisation and find a vehicle for the first sound film that would star Emil Jannings, also recently returned from Hollywood where he had been crowned with the first Academy Award ever conferred on an actor. One of the films for which he had received this award had been directed by the Austrian-born Josef von Sternberg; and after a more famous director, Ernst Lubitsch, had demanded a salary higher than UFA was prepared to pay, the more accommodating Sternberg was invited to see if his (admittedly uneasy) collaboration with Jannings could again be successful. The subject Jannings suggested, the life and death of Rasputin, did not interest Sternberg; Jannings therefore fell back on another, long-cherished project: to play the central part in an adaptation of Heinrich Mann's novel *Professor Unrat*. This concerned a high school teacher called Rath (pronounced 'Raat'), nicknamed 'Unrat' (filth) by the pupils he tyrannised, who fell in love with a chanteuse in a low waterfront dive called 'Der Blaue Engel', married her in defiance of what was expected from his class and calling, was dismissed from his post, and became a vengeful demon who used his wife to lure his fellow townsmen into gambling, dissipation and disgrace, until he is arrested for theft and thrown into gaol – distressing, no doubt, but alleviated by the satisfying feeling that he has had his revenge and fed his hatred of the society that had sought to cast him out.

This project faced two difficulties. The first of these was that media-Czar Alfred Hugenberg, who headed a largely like-minded UFA consortium, was also a leader of the right-wing German National People's Party; and that the author of *Professor Unrat* was a thorn in the side of that party, and of conservatives in the German film industry as a whole. Long before his involvement with the *Blue Angel* project, Heinrich Mann had become interested in the content and techniques of the silent film. Addressing a newly founded popular league for the encouragement of artistic film-making (Volksverband für Filmkunst) after the showing of Pudovkin's *The End of St Petersburg* in 1928, he called for German films that would emulate the Russians' ability to dramatise the work, social conditions, and mental set of large popular audiences; films that would not just be potboilers to make profit for the industry's moneymen, deliberate falsifications of what actually went on in the modern world, or escapist flights into remote ethereal regions. Such works might well be based on valuable literature, like Gerhart Hauptmann's *The Weavers*, recently filmed by Friedrich Zelnik. 'But why,' Mann concluded, 'does one need literature at all for this purpose? With material that has not passed through literary hands a film director can achieve even greater effects – if he is gifted enough. We do have such directors. They are eager to base their work, poetically, on the real nature of our time, to depict real figures in its atmosphere. Let them be allowed to go ahead! The Russian example shows how authentic unfalsified effects can be achieved.'[1]

The Soviet films praised in this passage were eagerly scanned by Josef Goebbels for pointers on how the cinema could be made an instrument for political propaganda – but since their propaganda sought to promote Soviet communism, they were anathema to Hugenberg and those who thought like him. Moreover, in novels like *Der Untertan* (*His Majesty's Loyal Subject*) Heinrich Mann had attacked aspects of the power and class structure of the Wilhelmine Empire that survived into the Republic; and in *Professor Unrat*, first published in 1905, he had used the popular form of the school story – usually reserved either for presenting the problems of adolescence and the clash of generations or for nostalgic recollection lightened by humour – for what Hugenberg and his like could only see as subversion of the established order.

Such subversion had, indeed, been part of the thrust of Mann's novel. It patently attacked, through its portrayal of a pedantic schoolmaster in charge of the central subjects of a German humanist Gymnasium (Classical and German literature), right-wing, nationalistic, militaristic attitudes in the Wilhelmine Empire, along with the Prussian school system with its fostering of fear and resentment, as well as narrow-minded, corruptible provincialism. Mann's description of his central protagonist is largely unsympathetic; it merges the idea of a lantern-jawed wooden puppet with images of animals like creeping cats and poisonous snakes. To add insult to injury, the object of his erotic passion turns out to be a rather stupid but good-natured petty-bourgeoise who supplements her income from singing in the lowest places of entertainment with occasional prostitution. Her marriage to the vengeful Unrat propels her into a demi-mondaine existence that involves tempting bored fellow townsmen into extravagances that lead to their ruin.

And here lay the second difficulty. If this novel were to be faithfully transferred to the screen, powerful professional bodies, like the German associations of high school teachers and academics, could be expected to resent such a portrayal of one of their number and agitate for a banning or picketing of the film, or at the very least attack UFA's policies and prestige.

How, then, could Klitzsch and Pommer sell this project to the UFA control board? They had two answers. One was that the central part would be tailored to an actor who had specialised in the portrayal of apparently strong, essentially sympathetic men brought down by fate, and by forces within themselves, to a fall which roused pity and terror in the audiences that had seen *Varieté*, *Der letzte Mann* (*The Last Laugh*) or the Sternberg-directed *The Last Command*. In that last instance, collaboration between director and star had been difficult, but they were both willing to do their best for the new project.

The second answer was that because of the considerable fee UFA was to pay – and the expectation of increased sales of a book that had not been a popular success – Mann had agreed to a radical alteration of his storyline from which political offence, and offence to professional bodies, would be removed. He had even agreed to a change of title: instead of the nickname of its central protagonist the film was to be given that of the low-class establishment which contained his nemesis.

'Zum Blauen Engel' had been the name of an ale-house in Carl Arnold Kortum's mock epic *Die Jobsiade* of 1784; but when Wilhelm Busch revived and illustrated these adventures of the theological candidate Jobs in 1872, the 'blue' angel had become a 'golden' one. Lübeck, however, the home town of the brothers Heinrich and Thomas Mann, still retained an inn called Zum Blauen Engel in the early part of the nineteenth century; Mann adopted this name but thought it appropriate to transfer it from a respectable part of town to an insalubrious side street leading off from the harbour. This activated the meaning of 'blau' as 'drunk, intoxicated', and 'blauer Montag' as the day after the weekend when no one feels like working. Sternberg's film accentuates this by having dissolute-looking putti floating around the stage on which Lola Lola absolves her turns and takes an occasional swig of beer.

There is, however, much more to this change of title. Theodor Adorno, who thought the film a travesty of a novel he admired, said that the new title suggested 'something about girls' ('Mädchen', which might also connote women of easy virtue); and sure enough, it did not take long before the 'blue angel' came to be thought of, not as the name of an inn, but as the description of an actress. And when that happened, the combination of 'blue' and 'angel' released a wholly different set of associations. The German Romantics had venerated blue as the colour of the heavens, the haze of distance which stimulated longings, and the blue mantle of the Sistine Madonna at Dresden, which had become a goal of Romantic pilgrimage. Novalis's *Heinrich von Ofterdingen* had enshrined 'the blue flower' as its central object of longing and had associated it with the feminine principle embodied in Sophie.

Speculations about the emotional effects of colour never ceased in the wake of the Romantic movement, whether in the writings of the painter Philip Otto Runge or those of the philosopher G. T. Fechner or Wilhelm Wundt's experiments with the dynamics of colour in the early twentieth century. What would have been freshest in the minds of the early audiences of Sternberg's film were the paintings and disquisitions of Wassily Kandinsky, who associated different shades of blue with different sounds made by musical instruments, and the blue horses in the paintings of Franz Marc. Indeed, when Kandinsky and Marc combined to edit a magazine in 1911, they called it *Der blaue Reiter* (*The Blue Horseman*). Considering that the cast of the film included one of Germany's most fashionable jazz bands, one may well speculate that for some knowledgeable contemporaries the blue of the angel may have brought to mind the 'mood indigo' of American jazz – especially the ubiquitous 'blues'. [2]

So it came about that the traditional name on a German inn-sign acquired multiple associations that soon wove themselves into the image of an actress who had appeared in many theatrical productions and had even had prominent roles in earlier German films, but who only became a star – some might say superstar – after Sternberg had cast her, against much vociferous opposition but loyally supported by Pommer, in *The Blue Angel*. After that Heinrich Mann's novel could be reissued, in the author's lifetime, under the title of the film rather than its original one, with the figure of a woman swathed in a blue scarf on its cover;[3] and a memorial essay on Dietrich in the German magazine *Der Spiegel* could appear under the title: 'Deutschlands ungeliebter Engel' – 'Germany's unloved angel'.[4]

2

TRANSFORMATIONS

The storyline which resulted from the compromises without which UFA would never have sanctioned turning Mann's novel into a film may be seen most clearly in the original trailer for the completed work which –

 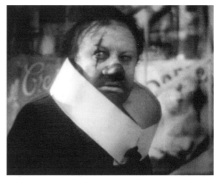

14   The professor before and after his fall

most unusually – gives away the plot. It is spoken, and has probably been composed, by Dr Hans Müller, one of UFA's screenplay doctors who assisted UFA's expert on the transformation of authors' manuscripts into usable screenplays, Robert Liebmann. Müller's spoken text is interspersed with key images from the film.

> Two worlds here confront each other: the stillness, earnestness, protected quiet atmosphere of an old small town – and against that the tumult, feverish nervousness, confusion and disorder of a low dockyard dive [Hafenspelunke]. In that first world of serious work lives a solitary man wholly dedicated to his profession of educating young people; the other world, however, a house of temptation, restlessness, frenzy, is ruled by —
>
> [Here the trailer intersperses a short sequence showing Lola singing her theme song.]
>
> The collision of these worlds results in fateful events that have often been seen before but are here made new and deeply moving: a solitary man filled with longings is broken by a mad illusion of love. We follow his fate through all its heights and depths. There is boisterous, high-spirited gaiety, but the seemingly happy encounter results in misunderstanding, jealousy and torment. Battling with his past, with the woman whose helpless subject he has become, with the judgement and prejudices of society, destroys this loving man and robs him of his human dignity. But then, summoning up the remnant of his strength, he drags himself away from hellish temptation. He staggers back into

Lola at the beginning of her relationship with the professor and at the end his solitude – and only now, with a broken heart, does he realise where his true happiness had lain. Over the lifeless body of the man purged of his guilt the central clock of this little, old, quiet town sounds once more its reverent tune: ÜB IMMER TREU UND REDLICHKEIT.[5]

It should occasion no surprise to find that discerning audiences should have their own views on Müller's valuations: that they might have different opinions on the professor's teaching methods and the nature of his code, based on a repetition of old tags that could hardly withstand inner drives and desires which compulsive behavioural patterns were in the end unable to keep suppressed. Nor would the woman, in face of whom his repressed sexuality breaks out, who propels him into a showbusiness world whose codes he can never adjust to, seem at all like a conventional vamp. Sternberg would hardly have been interested in remaking a cliché-ridden film like *The Way of All Flesh*.

To concoct the screenplay of *The Blue Angel* Pommer consulted Heinrich Mann (who approved of the alterations in public but complained in private) and brought together an editorial team composed of the novelist and playwright Carl Zuckmayer; the man-about-town Karl Vollmöller, a friend of Sternberg's and author of the kitsch scenario *The Miracle*, which Max Reinhardt's mammoth production helped to international success; the screenplay wizard Robert Liebmann (who also helped with song-texts); Pommer and (occasionally) Jannings – and Sternberg himself. The committee met, at first informally, in a Swiss alpine resort, but then, in a more businesslike atmosphere, in one of UFA's Berlin offices. They based their work on an adaptation of Mann's novel in *Novelle* form, scripted by Zuckmayer who made the agreed changes in Mann's plot and composed much of the dialogue. The committee then concocted a number of treatments and screenplays, two of which have survived, together with Zuckmayer's novella and a sheet of suggested alterations to an intermediate treatment which has not so far turned up again – and then handed the last of these scenarios, brought into acceptable screenplay form by Liebmann, to the director, who transposed, omitted and added essential scenes (including the wedding banquet, the professor's transformation into a clown, and silent observers essential to the film's sense of doom). Pommer sanctioned a shooting schedule in strict sequence – which increased costs, since sets that recurred later could not be dismantled – and obliged Sternberg to shoot each sequence first in German, then in English.

The survival of so many early stages of the screenplay, now happily reprinted by Discherl and Nickel in *Der blaue Engel. Die Drehbuchentwürfe*, offers an unusual insight into Sternberg's ultimate changes, made when he actually came to film what Robert Liebmann presented him with. It was he, for instance, who suggested – with a bow to Wedekind's Lulu, recently embodied by Louise Brooks in Pabst's *Die Büchse der Pandora* (*Pandora's Box*) – that the rather stupid Rosa Fröhlich, as she was named in Mann's novel and subsequent screenplay drafts – should be named Lola Lola, and tailored to fit Marlene Dietrich's intelligence and laid-back style.

Where the early treatments had made the chanteuse try to please audiences with songs beyond her capacity and education, distorting the opening words of Schubert's Serenade ('Leise flehen' – '[my songs] plead silently' into 'Läuse Flöhen' – 'lice and fleas'), Lola keeps absolutely within her range, and therefore does not go into hysterics over her audiences' lack of appreciation. Sternberg also tightened his film considerably by eliminating swathes of dialogue (the professor's gossiping housekeeper is reduced to three short lines and a few muttered words) and deleted whole scenes, like the conference of teachers which decides the professor's dismissal as well as the relegation of the three students whose attachment to Lola has lured their professor into the establishment in which she performs, and in which the correct bourgeois in his tight, formal clothes finds the embodiment of his sexual fantasies.

Though the action of the film is updated to 1925–9 from that of the original novel, which had been set in the Wilhelmine Empire, Sternberg eliminates the contemporary references in the screenplays submitted to him – such as the interjection by a scandalised spectator of the professor's humiliation: 'That's what comes of living in a Republic!' – and direct presentations of the class structure which had survived from the earlier period. The committee had envisaged a morning walk from the professor's house to his school in the course of which he is respectfully greeted by tradesmen (a greengrocer and a tobacconist), members of the judiciary (a clerk of court and a magistrate), a military man (a captain of the Reichswehr), a group of bankers, a traffic policeman, and a little flower-seller – all of whom turn away from him after his 'disgrace'. This becomes part of a tightening-up process which leads to the disappearance of several minor characters – a master butcher who attacks the professor, a publican's wife, an obnoxious black man, and others. Along with the elimination of scenes like an exciting honeymoon in Berlin, and the reduction of the 565 takes in the last extant screenplay to 506, these eliminations help to give *The Blue Angel* some of the feel of a *Kammerspielfilm*, the sparingly peopled stories in limited surroundings, which had been one of the genres favoured by Weimar film-makers in earlier days. Müller's retelling of the film's plotline should also have served to suggest the affinity of *The Blue Angel* with the 'street film' of Weimar Germany on which Fritz Lang, in *The Woman in the Window* and *Scarlet Street*, played characteristic variations in his Hollywood years. Such works dealt typically with the dangers that the streets outside – the wider world – held for buttoned-up bourgeois men lured out of their stuffy homes and secure professions by desires of the flesh and other, obscurer, longings for adventure.

While earlier scenarios had had the professor-turned-clown making hen-like noises when a stage magician conjures eggs from his nose, Sternberg invents a wedding banquet in which it is Lola who makes these noises while the professor answers her, to the delight of the showbusiness guests, with a series of cock-crows. It is the forced repetition of this turn when he becomes what the stage magician (who is also head of the troupe to which Lola belongs) calls, with a knowing wink at Goethe's famous ballad, 'August, mein Zauberlehrling' ('August, my Sorcerer's Apprentice'), which gives Jannings the chance to turn 'Kikeriki' into the terrifying cry of rage and despair when he tries to strangle the wife who had found a new and more satisfying lover in the strong man and escapologist Mazeppa. Sternberg clearly relished the irony that made the last sounds we hear from this once so articulate teacher of language and literature a horrible series of inchoate howlings. That he was turned from a professor of ancient Greek and German literature – an ideologically loaded subject in Germany's high school curriculum – into a teacher of English had much to do with the necessity of making an English-speaking version for the American and British market. Shakespeare's *Hamlet* and *Julius Caesar* therefore replaced Schiller's *Maid of Orleans* as subjects of instruction, and many classical allusions and linguistic mannerisms imported from the Greek, which had been taken over in early scenario drafts from Mann's novel, have disappeared in *The Blue Angel* Sternberg directed.

Lastly: Sternberg rejected clichéd 'absent-minded professor' traits introduced by the early scenarists; montage effects such as having a shot of chattering geese followed by another of gossiping women; and attempts at making the professor's hallucinations during his final walk visible by means of superimposed cinematic 'ghosts'. Inner processes were to be conveyed by facial expression and body language that the director sought to control as tightly as the physical environment he constructed around his actors to help determine the spirit and mood of each scene.

3
....
'SVENGALI JO' ASSEMBLES HIS TEAM

Emil Jannings (Theodor Friedrich Emil Janenz) seemed the ideal centre of UFA's prestige project. He had had a successful career in the theatre, so that no one needed to fear that his vocal powers would not be adequate to the early sound film; he had played important parts in silent films by some of Germany's most gifted directors; and the fame he had achieved in Hollywood promised profits abroad that justified high costs. He also had enough English to repeat his role in that language.

Josef von Sternberg (né Jonas Sternberg and known to George Grosz and other Berlin friends as 'Svengali Jo') was an autodidact in all fields except two: millinery, a minor branch of the rag trade in which he had served an apprenticeship, and the cinema, where he had graduated from mending film stock to film cutting and editing, assisting with screenplays and then writing them himself, acting as cameraman and assistant director, to fully-fledged directorial assignments in Hollywood. His career had had many downs as well as ups; and what commended him especially to Pommer and Klitzsch was that he had recently made a sound film, *Thunderbolt*, which had been well received.

Once Sternberg had agreed to come, UFA did him proud with a generous budget, a producer who promised him a free hand, and a team of writers, technicians and actors that included the best it had on offer. Fritz Thiery, in charge of the sound recording equipment, was the chief of UFA's new roster of sound experts. The principal cameraman Günther Rittau had gone through the hard school of Fritz Lang's epics *Die Nibelungen* and *Metropolis*, and had also worked with Joe May in the more confined spaces of *Asphalt*; he was seconded by a specialist for mountain films, suitably named Hans Schneeberger, who now brought to bear his experience with outdoor photography under Arnold Fanck and Leni Riefenstahl on the exclusively studio settings of *The Blue Angel*. Most experienced of all was the set designer and sculptor Otto Hunte: he had worked with Lang and Joe May since the former's *Der goldene See* (*The Golden Lake*) and the latter's *Die Herrin der Welt* in 1919, and had continued with both of them, working with May on *Das indische Grabmal* (*The Indian Tomb*) and with Lang on the *Mabuse* films, *Die Nibelungen*, *Metropolis*, *Spione* (*Spies*) and *Die Frau im Mond* (*The Woman in the Moon*); Pabst had also requested and obtained his services on the sets of *Die Liebe der Jeanne Ney* (*The Love of Jeanne Ney*). Sternberg was particularly grateful to him for the set of the dark street that leads from the day-time world of the professor's flat and school to the night-time world of the stage on which Lola, Kiepert, Guste and the rest exercise such skills and talents as they have. He became so fond of this set that he would not allow it to be struck until Pommer, for once, intervened behind his back and had it dismantled to free the studio stage concerned. Sternberg was also grateful to Hunte for the sculptured apostles on the town hall clock which looked forward to the equally grotesque figures Peter Balbusch designed for *The Scarlet Empress*. Hunte's colleague on the set design and construction team was Emil Hasler, who had served both Lang (on *Die Frau im Mond*) and Pabst (on the Louise Brooks vehicle *Tagebuch einer Verlorenen/Diary of a Lost Girl*) as recently as 1928–9. The costumes were designed by a Hungarian specialist called Tihamer Várady, who was omitted from the credits along with the painstaking make-up expert Waldemar Jabs, who has left an account of how he managed to suggest the stages of the professor's decline by successive alterations of his beard. Várady's costumes for Dietrich included a delicious parody of eighteenth-century formality, in which a courtly white wig on top was matched below by a hooped skirt transparent in front and cut away behind, affording yet another view of the frilled panties which form so essential an adjunct to Lola's stage act. The costume thus underlined the delightful elements of mockery and parody she introduced into what Kiepert calls her 'Schmalzkiste', her box of tricks.

After assigning such well-known writers as Carl Zuckmayer and Sternberg's friend, the globe-trotting Karl Vollmöller, to the project, alongside UFA's chief screenplay expert Robert Liebmann, to help the director with the construction of his film, the selection of suitable dialogue, and German language directions to focus-pullers, lighting experts, and other technicians, Erich Pommer also did his best to help him find actors who would fit his requirements and the roles they would be asked to play. Among these Jannings was a given – the project had been initiated by him and would ostensibly be built around him. Sternberg had seen ample proof of Jannings's talent for embodying apparently strong men brought down by some weakness in themselves, and the masochistic enjoyment he took in miming their consequent torment; this fitted well into the sado-masochistic pattern that marked so many of Sternberg's films, culminating in *The Devil Is a Woman*, his last film with Dietrich. He counteracted the physical bulk with which Jannings had dominated his earlier films, in which even his broad back had been celebrated for its expressive power, by casting as many fat actors around him as UFA could turn up – including an array of enormous women sitting on The Blue Angel stage in early sequences who seemed to have stepped out of paintings by George Grosz or Otto Dix. The fat publican who presides over The Blue Angel is played by Karl Huszar-Puffy, an actor of Hungarian extraction who had had parts in thrillers that included Lang's *Dr Mabuse, der Spieler* (*Dr Mabuse the Gambler and Player with People's Lives*) and had recently co-starred with Marlene Dietrich and Harry Liedtke in the film *Ich küsse Ihre Hand, Madame* (*I Kiss Your Hand, Madame*). He belonged to this same group of fatties Sternberg assembled around Jannings, as did a cabaret star with much film experience, Kurt Gerron, who played Kiepert, the stage magician and manager of Lola's troupe. Sternberg even has Gerron and Huszar-Puffy stand belly to belly

'You haven't exactly slimmed down since I saw you last!'

and compare their bulk. One of the functions of these characters was to set Dietrich's beauty into relief. Nor was her female co-star, Rosa Valetti, a threat to Dietrich in the beauty stakes; she too had had long experience playing character parts in films, including Ludwig Berger's *Das brennende Herz* (*The Burning Heart*) and Joe May's *Asphalt*. Like Gerron, she was also a key figure in the Berlin cabaret of the 1920s – of this something will be said later in this study.

Many of the other actors were hired after performances in the two most popular plays then running in Berlin: Georg Kaiser's play with music, *Zwei Krawatten* (*Two Neckties*) yielded Hans Albers, Rosa Valetti, and finally – Sternberg's own particular choice after much expert opposition – Marlene Dietrich; while Friedrich Wolf's *Cyankali*, which dealt with the problem of abortion and its illegality, yielded two important silent characters – a clown played by Reinhold Bernt, whose mute presence foreshadows the professor's ultimate fate and who may have been a predecessor in Lola's favours; and the school janitor, played by Hans Roth, who lights the professor's way back to his school platform and tries in vain to prise his dead hand away from a corner of his old desk. Two of the others, Eduard von Winterstein, as director of the school, and Wilhelm Diegelmann, as a drunken sea captain, were veterans of the German stage, with screen experience: the former, who

had been acting in films since 1911, was most recently seen as Blücher in Lupu Pick's *Napoleon auf Sankt Helena*, while the latter had been featured in a film version of Zuckmayer's circus comedy *Katharina Knie*, directed by Karl Grune and released in 1929. It was Zuckmayer too who had insisted on the casting of his friend Hans Albers, writing

The janitor (left), the school director

the part of Mazeppa with his particular voice and way of speaking firmly in mind. Albers had been an athletic variety artist and had played elegant or dubious characters in a multitude of silent films but it was not until sound came along that his real career as 'der blonde Hans, der Sieger', the German hero *par excellence*, took off, helped as much by his rough singing voice as by his Hamburg-toned, popular manner of speaking.

Particular care had been taken about the casting of the boys: Angst, the professor's star pupil, whose name indicated his timid attitude to authority, and the three rebellious boys whose precocious sexual interest

Angst, the professor's favourite

led the professor to pursue them into Lola's sphere of enchantment. Their very appearance had to suggest the difference in their natures. The aptly named Angst was played by Rolf Müller, who had recently been praised by critics for his acting in Carl Boese's *Geschminkte Jugend* (*Young People with Make-up*) of 1929. The most elegant and blasé of the rebellious trio, Rolant Varno, had played the lead in a film called *Jugendtragödie* (*Tragedy of Youth*), and had been cast as a schoolboy in two other films about the problems of adolescents. In one of these, *Zwischen vierzehn und sechzehn* (*Between Fourteen and Sixteen*), directed by E. W. Emo, he had been joined by Robert Klein-Lörk, a young veteran of the popular Stuart Webbs series of action films, who was chosen to play Goldstaub – a Jewish scamp such as had been made popular by Ernst Lubitsch in early Jewish farces like *Schuhpalast Pinkus* (*Shoe Emporium Pinkus*). The equivalent character in Mann's novel had not been Jewish, and Klein-Lörk's all too efficient portrayal of sneaky *chutzpe* may well have brought some fuel to the anti-Semitic fires that were to turn into a

The three precocious visitors to
The Blue Angel

conflagration three years after the release of *The Blue Angel* and lead to
the withdrawal of a film that had so much Jewish talent both behind and
before its cameras.

The last of the young men cast as boys in Sternberg's film had
earned high critical praise for his part in Georg Asagaroff's *Revolte im
Erziehungshaus* (*Revolt in a House of Correction*) and had played the
leading part of Moritz Stiefel in Richard Oswald's film version of
Wedekind's *Frühlings Erwachen* (*Spring's Awakening*), released in 1929.
His name was Karl Balhaus; he had to mime the slow learner, product of
the country gentry, who is at the receiving end of the professor's
endeavours to teach his pupil the proper way of pronouncing the English
'th' – aided by much mutual emission of spittle and the insertion of a
pencil between the unfortunate boy's teeth.

Sternberg was a member of the team that worked on the various
scenarios, and after it had dispersed Pommer left him in sole charge to
alter, transpose or otherwise transmute what had been worked out. This
applied also to his choice of the leading actress, against expert advice and
formidable competition. Marlene Dietrich often reiterated, in later life,
how much she owed to him; what he said about this is that all he had done
was to recognise what was in her, and dramatise *that* with the magic of
light and shade. Here he pointed to something which is often overlooked
when anecdotes about his directorial ways are rehashed, and when one
considers his frequent assertion that he used actors as colours on his
palette or notes in his compositions. He had a strongly empathetic streak
which recognised in Dietrich not only her sexuality, but also a
motherliness that went with it, and a Prussian sense of duty and
obligation which not only made her an ideal colleague to work with, but

could be used for her characterisation of Lola, who knows and accepts the discipline showbusiness imposes on those who have to make their living by courting public favour, while her depressed husband can't accept showbusiness codes or respect the public from which Kiepert's troupe earns its – and his – bread. Above all Sternberg valued in Dietrich a relaxed attitude quite different from Prussian *Schneidigkeit*, clipped sharpness, and Prussian attitudes to authority. In a male-dominated world she knows how to defuse pompous authority. With delightful Berlinese she punctures bluster from those who claim superiority by virtue of being (as they announce themselves) 'Doctor Immanuel Rath, Professor at the Gymnasium of this town' or 'Kiepert, Magician and Director'. But Dietrich also knew how to pay respect when it was due, and never failed to give due credit to the director who brought out the full force of her talent and personality.

Sternberg understood Jannings just as well as Dietrich, and has left a most amusing portrait of his gluttony, childish tantrums, and egocentricity without minimising his abilities as an actor who took a masochistic delight in miming suffering and humiliation. This found a ready response, not only in Germans humiliated by the Versailles Treaty and the tribulations that followed, but also in Sternberg himself, who had known humiliations enough in his own life and career. A keen observer like Dietrich's daughter Maria noticed this at once when she was introduced to 'a stocky little man with a big droopy moustache and the saddest eyes I had ever seen'. Ever afterwards she thought of him as 'a man easily embarrassed, vulnerable, unsure', who spent much energy 'pretending just the opposite, always trying to hide what he believed to be his weaknesses'.[6] In Jannings's case, Sternberg built some of the form which his humiliation should take around a private quirk:

> Jannings was extremely partial to ... birds, and his rooms were full of ... squawking parrots, and chirpers from his native forests, among them one whistler known as Pinkus whom he consulted on all financial matters. At the back of his garden was a chicken coop and confined to this annex were Greta Garbo, Pola Negri, Valentino, Jack Gilbert, Conrad Veidt, Lya de Putti, and other clucking hens and crowing roosters named after the many visitors who achieved this distinction after bringing a tribute of sausages.[7]

Out of this grew the dead bird at the beginning of *The Blue Angel* – not an exotic canary, but a bullfinch 'from his native forests' – which is so miraculously 'resuscitated' in Lola's bedroom; and more particularly the 'crowing rooster' turn at the wedding feast and repeated in very different ways and circumstances during the final humiliation of the professor turned reluctant stooge, clown and cuckold.

Of greatest importance in the casting of *The Blue Angel*, after the imaginative choice of Dietrich for the professor's wet dream, was the appointment of Friedrich Hollaender to preside over the musical side of what The Blue Angel stage offered its public. Hollaender was a classically trained composer from a family prominent in German literary, theatrical and musical life, and had helped to make the sophisticated cabaret (and cabaret-revue) one of the glories of Berlin in the 1920s. He not only composed melodies that quickly became *Schlager* (hit songs), reaching beyond cabaret and film through the burgeoning radio and gramophone industry, but he also wrote texts for his own songs and those of others, directed shows conceived by himself, and played piano accompaniments without swamping the singers' voices. He brought with him into the cast of *The Blue Angel* one of the leading German jazz groups of the time, led by Stefan ('Steps') Weintraub, and known as the Weintraubs-Syncopators. In the film Hollaender and the Weintraubs appear as The Blue Angel's resident musicians.

Friedrich Hollaender among the Weintraubs-Syncopators

A last word about Dietrich, the clearest illustration of the old showbusiness adage that it takes ten years to make an overnight success. Contrary to her own repeated denials she had made named appearances in fourteen previous films, four of them in leading parts noticed (and usually praised) by contemporary reviewers, had been cast in speaking parts in plays by Shakespeare, Shaw and important modern German playwrights like Georg Kaiser, and had attracted Berlin's attention in cabarets and revues – most notably in *Es liegt in der Luft* (*It's in the Air*) by Marcellus Schiffer and Mischa Spolinsky, in which she had sung a trio with Margo Lion and Oskar Karlweis which had lesbian overtones and a catchy tune immediately picked up by gramophone and radio. There had been glimpses of what Dietrich was to become under Sternberg's direction, lighting and make-up instruction in Kurt (later Curtis) Bernhardt's *Die Frau, nach der man sich sehnt* (*The Woman One Longs For*), in which she had played the lead opposite Fritz Kortner, who was then at the height of his power and fame. Nevertheless, it was under Sternberg's aegis that Marlene became a star – the only truly international filmstar born in Germany.

It has often been noticed how many key members of the *Blue Angel* team – Albers, Valetti, Gerron, Dietrich, Hollaender, the Weintraubs – had cabaret and revue experience; but that has led to a mistaken identification of the Blue Angel stage show as that of a 'cabaret' or 'nightclub'. It is nothing of the kind: it is a beer hall and rough eating-house, in which people order food and drink while the stage show is going on, and where customers yell out to Lola that they have their wage-packet with them ('Hier sitzt die Lohntüte') presumably for special favours

The rowdy interior of The Blue Angel

which she is not likely to grant. She takes it all in good part, and goes on with her performance regardless of interruptions. The fat ladies of the chorus are firmly told by their director that they must go on drinking beer in order to stimulate the customers to do likewise. When the professor calls Kiepert 'elender Kuppler' – wretched procurer – he suspects that

The Blue Angel is a knocking shop on the side, what early critics called a 'Hafenbumslokal' (a dockside dive where prostitution goes on). The cabaret-and-revue-honed members of Sternberg's cast are slumming here; but they could do so in style, because impersonations of poor and working-class figures, of the kind the artist Heinrich Zille drew, were a staple part of the repertoire of sophisticated cabaret artists in the 1920s. One of the screenplays antecedent to the film's continuity had envisaged a *Zillekind* as one of its characters; this ultimately disappeared, but the little girl who delivers the milk for the professor's breakfast at the film's beginning is a fair approximation.

What The Blue Angel's public is offered is not the kind of cabaret or revue that Dietrich and the others were used to, but a downmarket variety show which includes a conjurer, gymnasts, a dancing bear, as well as solo and chorus singing – and two kinds of clown. Sternberg himself seems to have forgotten, in later life, that both figured in his staging: a sad-faced man with a crumpled face, wearing a fez-like hat, who appears constantly in the professor's path; an early version of the screenplay calls him 'der Trottel', the Clumsy Fool. The other clown, who also gazes sadly at the professor, is an Auguste; he wears the red nose, wide collar and heavy make-up the professor will later have to don himself. It is this Auguste figure that Kiepert uses in his act – we hear him berate his unfortunate

assistant for bringing him the wrong props. I thought at one time that they might be the same actor in different make-up – but the two of them appear together in one shot that is clearly not produced by trick photography.

It is probably the distance between the sophisticated cabarets and revues that she frequented as well as appeared in which made Dietrich, in her autobiographical reflections issued under the title *Nehmt nur mein Leben* ..., report that she thought, at times, that the film in which Sternberg had cast her was 'recht ordinär' – rather vulgar.[8] She thought above all that the cameras – four at a time at one juncture – were trained too exclusively on her legs. Heinrich Mann, however, who appreciated the increased revenue that the adaptation of *Professor Unrat* had brought him, and who loyally defended the altered title and altered plotline he had agreed to when talking to Pommer and Zuckmayer, voiced fundamental doubts in a letter to a friend, and was heard to remark, in private, that the success of *The Blue Angel* was in large measure due to Miss Dietrich's naked thighs.[9]

4

. . . .

ARTIFICIAL GARDENS, REAL TOADS

Sternberg arrived in Berlin on 16 August 1929, and left again, after completing the editing of the German version of his first and only German film, on 11 February 1930. This was a truly fateful period for the Weimar Republic. Having weathered the worst monetary inflation in history, and started economic recovery despite the crippling burden of 'reparations' imposed by the Versailles Treaty, the German economy was plunged into decline by the US stock-market crash on Black Friday, 25 October 1929. There were bank failures, cancellations of orders and defaults on payment, and the number of the unemployed among white collar as well as blue collar workers rose dramatically. Resentment of the Versailles terms, and of the 'war guilt' clause that underpinned them, was not eased by the Young Plan which sought to spread the reparations over a wider period, reducing annual payments and arranging for foreign loans to cover them. The newly formed Nazi party, NSDAP, profited by these discontents; in tandem with Hugenberg's National People's Party and other right-wing organisations, they tried to force a referendum that would reject the Young Plan and renege on the peace terms. This did not succeed, but it raised the profile of Hitler's party, and led to its increased success in elections to the governments of the various *Länder* into which the Republic's administration was divided. Industrialists and bankers saw the way the wind was blowing, and increasingly financed the NSDAP. To complete the Republic's misfortunes its most capable statesman, Gustav

Stresemann, died of exhaustion in 1929; another, Walter Rathenau, had been assassinated by anti-Semitic agitators seven years earlier. Popular xenophobia was little assuaged by the British evacuation of the occupied Rhineland: it only made the French occupation of industrial heartlands all the more resented, while at the same time anti-Semitic campaigns waged by journals like Goebbels's *Völkischer Beobachter* were fuelled by a widely reported financial scandal centring on the activities of the brothers Sklarek.

In his autobiography Sternberg revealed how sensitive he was to the atmosphere around him in the Berlin of 1929. The burdens placed on defeated Germany by the victors of 1918, he tells his readers, and bitter memories of an inflation which had impoverished the many but enriched the few, had led to a seething Berlin in which 'moral values had become obsolete'. 'It would be wrong to suppose,' he continues, 'that all of the city was in hectic pursuit of questionable values, but enough was in sight to give that impression … Outwardly Berlin in 1929 was an evocation by Goya, Beardsley, Marquis de Bayros, Zille, Baudelaire and Huysmans.'[10]

Some of that spirit has crept into *The Blue Angel*, with its overt sexuality – though that seems to owe more to Félicien Rops and Toulouse-Lautrec than the artists just named – and its sado-masochism. How much more cruel the schoolboys are than their resented master, once the latter has become vulnerable! The last words spoken in the film are by Kiepert, who promises 'to make everything all right again' ('alles wieder in Ordnung bringen') after his clown's murderous onslaught accompanied by inarticulate cries of rage and pain; but the last word sung is the sharply articulated word 'garnichts' – 'nothing at all' – followed by the professor's wordless death and the striking of the midnight hour by the town hall clock whose chorale-like tune plays so important a part in the structure of the film.

It was, however, one of Sternberg's most deeply held beliefs that the kind of artist he saw himself as – an *auteur avant la lettre* – constructed cinematic worlds that had little in common with the everyday world around him. His was a world of psychological rather than historic truth, of moods and feelings rather than social realities, conjured up by skilful deployment of the camera, of gradations of light and shade, of hundreds of deliberately chosen and placed objects within an approved set design. His favourite metaphors to describe his activity included that of a painter who used the camera as his brush, a musician who used actors and equally important physical props as so many notes in his compositions, a poet who alters the scripts he is given until they meet 'my standards of visual poetry',[11] and a cold-eyed mechanic who built precise constructions with the help – but often, alas, against the resistance – of the many others concerned in the making of a given film.

In 1929 the still rather primitive Klangfilm sound equipment meant that vision and sound had to be recorded together, that the cameraman – and a camera-conscious director – had to be enclosed in a soundproof box, and that therefore 'liberated camera' effects like those pioneered by Karl Freund in Murnau's *The Last Laugh* were impossible until the advent of dubbing techniques and other technical improvements already present in American studios. Nevertheless Sternberg and his UFA team welcomed the possibility of adding soundtracks to hitherto 'silent' film because it brought cinematic art nearer to the *Gesamtkunstwerk*, the 'total work of art' of which the Romantics had dreamed and which Wagner had sought to fulfil in his own way at Bayreuth. Sternberg was also thrilled by the idea that sound would open up new possibilities of effective silences in the same way as every light brought with it its own shade.

After the musically accompanied credit sequence, which will be examined in the next section, Sternberg fades in a long shot from above onto steeply gabled roofs with smoking chimneys which immediately propel us into what might be called UFALAND – the archaic settings constructed in the studio by the designers of films like *The Student of Prague* or *Faust: A German Folktale*. Though a later sequence shows that the action of *The Blue Angel* has been updated from Mann's 1905 to 1925–9, this very opening shot takes the spectator away from any actual German town like Lübeck to a constructed world like that of the imagined Russia or China or Spain of Sternberg's later films with Dietrich. The Expressionistic design of the crooked street through which the professor passes on his way to The Blue Angel tavern has been preserved – its realisation in the film takes us even deeper into the world of Wiene or Leni, film-makers Sternberg singles out for praise, along with Murnau, Dupont and Joe May, in his autobiography. When the camera shows us Jannings hurrying through this street enveloped in the cloak he wears outdoors, his back view distinctly suggests Caligari on nefarious business in Holstenwall.

The remoteness of the *Blue Angel* world from that of the real Germany of 1925–9 is strengthened by the absence of motor cars, gramophones, radios and even – if the many posters liberally posted up all over the place in the Blue Angel dressing rooms, bedrooms, corridors as well as outside walls are any guide – the cinema. The drunken sea captain has just arrived from Calcutta on a *sailing* vessel, and most of the lamps that hang down or stand up so liberally in set after set seem to burn gas. The exception is the light in Lola's dressing room,

Sternberg's use of posters

where the circular shade and bulb strengthen the circular motif of black and white top-hats hanging side by side on hooks, the chair on which Lola spins the professor round, the many round bottles and jars on the make-up table, and even Kiepert's large round face, on which a plastered-down forelock adds an oval to the overall circularity. It is Lola too who, treating the professor like a child, sends him out into the street

The professor obstructed by nets

with the warning to beware of 'die Elektrische' – but this reference to electric tramcars hardly dispels our sense that we are in UFALAND rather than in Lübeck or some other actual town of the 1920s. The English versions substitute a warning about 'banana-skins'.

Sternberg loves dimming his images of people or places through low-key lighting, shadows, the interposition of smoke from chimneys, cigars or cigarettes, nets, water thrown against a display window, steamed up or soiled window panes, a cloud of powder blown against a face, objects dangling from ceilings or rearing up in front and partial masking of the lower edges of his shots. All this creates a dream-like atmosphere which further increases the viewer's sense of strangeness, disorientation – of being precipitated into an alternative world.

In this artificial world, however, real passions are enacted. What Sternberg and his team give us is, in Marianne Moore's words, 'imaginary gardens with real toads in them'. It is a deliberately dense world, crowded with objects that have real uses but also – like the dredge in Sternberg's early film *The Salvation Hunters* – symbolic import. In *The Blue Angel* these include the caged bird dead in the first sequence and burned in a stove, but phoenix-like 'revived' in Lola's bedroom, with its obvious connotations of sexual satisfaction; and also the doves that besiege the town hall clock. Other such objects are the nets and curtains that impede the professor's progress in The Blue Angel, the ship's naked figurehead rearing up below the box from which he watches Lola's performance, and the anchor that hangs down before her while she sings – things which, like the mournful ships' sirens that sound through the dark streets, suggest a *harbour* without the wider vista of an open sea traversed by ships that would have broken through the film's deliberate claustrophobia. They also, of course, add to the emotional colouring that is so important in this work. The professor's Strindbergian confinement in a straitjacket is only a stronger version of his earlier entanglements in nets, curtains and secret sexual fantasies. The narrowest confinement is still to come: his rigid dead body and the 'cool grave' of which the town hall clock's carillon speaks to him throughout the film.

Every object seen in *The Blue Angel* is there because the director wanted it there; nothing comes before the camera accidentally. Sternberg abominated what he called 'dead space' between the camera eye and the actors, and he filled this in with a profusion of props. At the same time, however, he wanted to stimulate imagination by concealing parts of his set: through objects looming into the frame from above or below, or double framing it with stove-pipes or screens or pillars, or draping gauze over part of it. He liked to light his sets in the manner of Claude Lorrain or Caspar David Friedrich, with a shadowy foreground, brighter lit middle ground, and brightest illumination at the back, drawing the spectator deeper into the picture through long shots and then exploring the space through varying medium shots of details in it. But there is a crucial difference between the effect achieved in the paintings of Claude, and even more those of Friedrich, and Sternberg's *mise en scène*. In the former the eye is led to the open sky, which for Friedrich holds the promise of another, better world, to which the foreground figures turn their eyes; Sternberg on the other hand closes his world off, with stage sets that terminate in tatty backcloths, with low-key lighting, and all manner of constriction that impedes full vision. The effect of closure gained in this way is enhanced, of course, by the fact that everything is studio-bound, studio-constructed, from the gabled UFA roofs at the beginning to the dark schoolroom at the end, where a solitary circle of light falls on a dead man whose face we cannot see. That action takes place predominantly in the middle ground enhances the constricted effect: characters seem pinned between whatever fills foreground and background, hemmed in by a profusion of things standing around: screens, heaped-up books, posters covering the whole surface of a wall, garments hanging about or draped over a piece of furniture. When there are close-ups, they are generally of objects rather than faces: the professor's name-plate, the town hall clock, the postcards fanned out in the professor's hand like playing cards, the calendar marking the lapse of

years from 1925 to 1929. This last instance also offers one of the rare examples of changes by means of the superimposition of images – others occur during the milk delivery sequence at the beginning, and during the procession, thematically so important, of grotesque apostle figures as the town hall clock strikes the hours and plays the musical injunction that enjoins the good burghers to faithfulness and honesty.

In the German version of *The Blue Angel* Sternberg kept a tight control on the cutting and editing process. He structured his film like a string of pearls: one carefully composed sequence leads to the next, each advancing the action in some significant way. Transitions are usually made by fade out / fade in, or by straight cuts from one sequence to the next. Such cuts lend themselves to ironic effects: we hear the professor announce repeatedly that he will take up the matter of his students' peccadilloes again, but events prevent him from ever doing so; or he declares categorically that as long as he has a penny left, saucy postcards of his wife will never again be sold to the public, only to appear, in the very next scene, hawking these same postcards around a public he despises, and complaining that he sold only two. Sound occasionally anticipates the next scene before the previous one has quite disappeared. A significant example occurs when the professor furtively blows on the postcard photo of Lola which has feathers pasted on to it, masking Lola's thighs until they are exposed when the feathers are blown on. The Blue Angel music is heard before the next shot showing Lola on her stage – the music seems therefore to emanate from the photo in the professor's hand. Sternberg was an expert on feathers, lace, frills and furbelows, and used such things as emblems of femininity in several films. The character played by Evelyn Brent in *Underworld* is actually called 'Feathers McKoy', and Sternberg claims that he even had feathers sown onto her underwear.

A significant example of Sternberg's use of cinematic space is afforded by the long shot that follows the opening view of gabled roofs: a marketplace with dark bales and baskets in the front, action of women loading chattering geese in the middle ground, with a side street leading into the market at the left, where we can discern a market stall before a shed, houses with ladders on which people are cleaning windows, two women talking with each other just visible at the centre, and, mostly clearly recognisable in the background on the right, a woman cleaning a shop door while in the middle ground a lamp post and a leaning frame of some kind partly impede the view. This space is then explored when a medium shot

The opening sequence

shows the woman who had cleaned the glass door cranking the handle that raises the window blind. A closer shot then lets us see the blind going up like a stage curtain, revealing a sexually provocative poster of 'Lola Lola' with a putto clinging to her leg. The woman then partially obscures the view by throwing a bucketful of water against the pane, and as the watery veil gradually clears away, we see the woman look at the poster and then try to imitate the titillating stance portrayed. This gives us the first of many glances directed towards Lola; significantly, it is an admiring female glance to balance the many male ones Lola invites through the way she makes her living – most significantly, of course, those of the professor. It is important to realise, however, that Lola gives as good as she gets, selecting by glances of her own, aided in one crucial sequence by a spotlight she directs at the professor who will be her future (very unsuitable) husband. When she encounters, in Mazeppa, a sexually and temperamentally more adequate partner who knows the rules of her own showbusiness world, their glances meet with equal frankness; and in her deflating replies to Kiepert, the director of the troupe whose star she is, she shows a pleasing ability to hold her own and preserve her dignity when men presume to order her around.

In the later part of the film close-ups of *faces* at last supplement the earlier close-ups of *objects*: the grotesque face of the professor in full Auguste make-up, after we have watched him slowly applying the mask in front of one of the many mirrors that double and hem in the characters who frequent the dressing rooms of the showbusiness world, is all the more powerful because we have had to wait so long; the same is true of the cheek-to-cheek close-up of Lola and her new lover, which leads to the professor's emerging from depression and anomie into inchoate jealous rage, until he finally drags himself to his death.

A characteristic example of Sternberg's *mise en scène* is afforded by the establishing shot of the Blue Angel stage, with the audience darkly at the front, the landlord in the immediate middle ground below the stage, the stage itself with Lola in its front portion, a dark anchor hanging before her and a stuffed seagull below, fat women sitting in a semicircle behind her, and in the rear in the farthest reach of the camera-eye, a backcloth with a painted sun and the establishment's trademark angels. The lighting is so managed that the spectator's glance is drawn to the rear of the set; this has been sprayed with water on Sternberg's orders so that the painted sun would bounce the light back while an overhead spotlight weaves a halo around Lola's hair. Part of a curtain or flat hangs down from the top on the righthand side of the stage, matching the dark mass of spectators in the front.

Important though this stage set is, however, especially when it is explored during Lola's songs, the really central space is Lola's dressing room into which all the main characters, and some minor ones, sooner or

Close-ups of faces

later penetrate. It has a winding staircase leading up to the heaven of Lola's bedroom, and a trapdoor precipitating into a hell in which the errant boys and their pursuing teacher have their unhappy encounter. It has doors that lead into the beer hall, others that lead to the dressing room into which the minor players have to cram their bulk, and another door that leads onto the stage. When these open, raucous noises and music penetrate into the place of transformation in which the professor is treated like a schoolboy and later changed into an Auguste, and in which Lola exhibits charms that are sometimes half-hidden by a folding screen, sometimes half-revealed by mirrors.

Mirrors serve many functions in Sternberg's films; in *The Blue Angel* they are an essential adjunct to Lola, whose living depends to a large extent on the appearance she can create by means of theatrical make-up. Perhaps the most interesting instance, however, occurs when it is not Lola but the professor who sits at the make-up table and checks in the mirror his

The professor besieged at the make-up table

progressive transformation into an Auguste. The audience in the cinema gets to watch not only that process, as it appears to him, but also the simultaneous growth of intimacy between Lola and the virile Mazeppa. We see the nascent Auguste look down as Lola and Mazeppa loom over him – and at the same time we notice that Mazeppa, standing on Lola's left, is reflected by the mirror on her right, making it appear, to the professor as to us, that Lola is besieged by putative lovers from both sides, doubly threatening him with cuckoldry at the moment of his deepest depression.

A master of light like Sternberg will inevitably be sensitive to the uses of shadow too; and in at least one place in *The Blue Angel*, the scene in which boys break into the bedroom of the professor's star pupil to punish him for 'snitching', he deliberately harks back to the shadow world of German silent film. Before we can make out the intruders into the dimly lit room we see their shadows on the wall, creeping towards

Shadows on the wall

their victim with arms outstretched like Cesare about to murder Alan in *Das Cabinet des Dr. Caligari* (*The Cabinet of Dr Caligari*).

The technical staff assigned to him by Pommer abetted Sternberg's attempts to make this prestigious German sound film approach the Romantic and Wagnerian ideal of the total work of art as nearly as possible. He used every variety of sound: animal noises (geese, a cat), different timbres of the human voice, gradations of speech from the pedantically distinct to muttered complaints, whistling, song, instrumental music including ensemble playing as well as solo piano and clarinet, bells, glockenspiel, music box effects coming out of a black doll,

One of many channels of visual communication

sirens. He uses every channel of visual communication too: lettering, printed posters with Rops-like drawings, paintings or photographs, risqué postcards, caricatures drawn with chalk, stage sets and sets that stylise the world beyond the stage, costumes ranging from Rath's tight formal clothes to Lola's transparent dresses and frivolous underclothes, mirror images. All these act as a language just as much as speech or the sudden advent of a degree of silence that belies the naturalism of the sounds that preceded it.[12]

In his autobiography Sternberg explained the relative immobility of his camera – compared with a horizon of expectations opened up by such silent masterpieces as *The Last Laugh* – by describing the constriction imposed on director and focus-puller when vision and sound had to be recorded at the same time in UFA's Babelsberg studios.[13] The fact, however, that the camera moves comparatively little in most sequences throws into relief scenes in which such movement does occur. The salient instance is the slow backward track from the professor

The tracking movement gains
tragic force

gathering his things together at his platform, over the schoolboys' empty
desks, towards the back of the schoolroom, after his career there has
come to its sudden end. This same tracking movement is duplicated in the
same schoolroom at the conclusion of the film; but this time the daylight
of the first occurrence is replaced by nocturnal gloom broken by the
circle of light (from a forgotten lantern) thrown onto the dead
professor's bowed head and clutching hand. Nothing could more
economically suggest the inevitability of the fate of *this* professor as
against that depicted in Heinrich Mann's original novel in which the
tyrant becomes a vengeful anarchist.

When Sternberg authorised a translation of the German continuity
for the London firm of Lorrimer Publishing, he contributed a preface in
which he tried to define, once again, 'the director's function, if he is to
function'.

It embraces a skill in all the arts, though this in itself means little. Every step and every moment is filled with imponderables. Trifles light as air must be ready to become substantial. An audience of one, he controls the camera according to his vision, uses light, shadow and space as his mind dictates, dominates the tempo and content of sound, controls the sets, chooses and edits the actors, decides their appearance and make-up, arranges the scenes in rhythmic progression, eliminates and adds moments that have no meaning to those who stand in attendance, and is solely responsible for every frame of his film. Aside from that he is chief of his crew of workmen, often numbering hundreds though it were better if he managed the giant task of harnessing the cumbersome machine by himself alone. That was my task and this I intended to do.[14]

UFA gave him a freedom to pursue that task to a degree he was never to achieve again until his last film, *The Saga of Anatahan*, made in Japan; a unique film but a solitary one, never destined to anything like the public impact, or indeed the public debate about its merits and demerits, of his first and only German film.

5
....
'TENDING TOWARDS MUSIC':
CONTRAST AND COUNTERPOINT

In the month after *The Blue Angel* had opened in Berlin, and while working on a film he directed himself, Friedrich Hollaender published an essay on music in sound films ('Die Musik im Tonfilm – Reichsfilmblatt', 10 May 1930). 'By their own nature,' he wrote, 'the concrete and abstract events depicted in a film always tend towards music.' 'Their development,' he added, 'can even be materially advanced and refined by musical structuring. I myself tested this insight when composing the music for *The Blue Angel*. The director of that film, von Sternberg, an exceedingly sensitive artist, was so clear about his own task, that he wished to get to know my compositions before beginning his work in the studio. He expected the music to fertilise his own creative endeavours.' In what follows Hollaender uses such terms as 'Leitmotiv' and 'Schicksalsmotiv' which are common currency in discussions of Wagner's operas.[15]

And it is indeed Wagner who presides over the music played as the title and opening credits unroll on the screen – more particularly the overture to *Tannhäuser*, with its interplay and variation of two contrasting themes. In Hollaender's composition the solemn striking of a bell announcing the hour is followed by what Hollaender calls the professor's fate motif: a tune to which every German could supply the words of a constantly taught and reiterated poem by Friedrich Hölty, whose opening line had recently formed the title of a silent film:

Üb immer Treu und Redlichkeit,	Be ever faithful, ever honest,
Bis an dein kühles Grab,	Until you come to your cold grave,
Und weiche keinen Finger breit	And do not stray a hair's breadth
Von Gottes Wegen ab.	From godly paths.

The lines of the poem which follow this passage are equally relevant: they bring in the notion of 'pilgrimage' which links this theme to *Tannhäuser*'s pilgrim's chorus: 'Then, they proclaim, you will tread the pilgrim's path through life as over green meadows; and then you can look death in the face without fear and trembling.'

Against this theme (Hollaender calls it a 'chorale') creeps another that corresponds to the Venusberg motif of Wagner's opera: a slow waltz that will soon be associated with a song known in German as 'Von Kopf bis Fuss' and in English as 'Falling in Love Again' – Lola's theme song, in fact, which Hollaender describes as a 'chanson' and 'Schlager', as well he might, for the gramophone and radio had already made it widely known and appreciated. These themes intertwine, Lola's growing ever stronger, though we still hear the professor's when the overture comes to an end. In the film the tag 'Üb immer Treu und Redlichkeit' associates itself with other mottoes the bourgeois professor tries to live by: 'Tue recht und scheue niemand' ('Act justly and fear no one') framed over his bed, and 'Ora et labora' inscribed over the front entrance of the school in which he teaches. The full import of Lola's tune won't be realised until we hear her sing this and the other songs Hollaender and Liebmann wrote for her; and the subversion hidden in the professor's key-tune becomes clearer when we see the town hall clock which constantly chimes it out and the doves which sit and fly about the town hall's roof. Alert audiences will then wake up to the fact that the tune in question is in fact an adaptation of one of Papageno's songs in *The Magic Flute* in which 'doves' stand for 'maidens':

Ein Mädchen oder Weibchen	A girl or a little wife
Wünscht Papageno sich,	Papageno wishes himself,
Ja, so ein holdes Täubchen	For such a dear little dove
Wär Seligkeit für mich.	it would be bliss to have.

So the erotic lurks within the straitlaced injunction.

Once we have been alerted to this we begin to realise that much of the music naturalistically introduced into the film tells us of the professor's state of mind – secret wishes and secret fears of which he may not be conscious himself before succumbing to them in the alien world of a waterfront dive. The tune he whistles to his songbird, for instance, before he knows it is dead, belongs to a ditty that speaks of longing and forced separation:

Ach, wie ist's möglich dann	O, how is it possible
Dass ich dich lassen kann …	that I could leave you …

– traditional words whose full application can only be appreciated when the housekeeper unfeelingly picks up the dead bird and throws it into the stove, and when, in Lola's bedroom, another caged bird chirps merrily away. The nineteenth-century poem on which this tune is based bears the significant title 'Treue Liebe', 'Faithful Love' – so that once again love is lurking within the professor's signature tune: 'Üb immer *Treu* und Redlichkeit'.

What we may now call 'the professor's music' is next heard sounding in the classroom. While the boys are puzzling over a trick question he has assigned as their essay subject, he opens a window and hears voices from a nearby girls' school singing another traditional song of love always known as 'Ännchen von Tharau', although the original poem, by Simon Dach, was entitled 'Der Palmbaum', 'The Palm Tree'. 'Little Anna from Tharau is the one I love / She is my life, my goods, my wealth.' Once the professor has pounced on Lola's photo, however, and impounded two more, Lola's music will counter his – in the German but not the English versions, the photos are unseen until a close-up shows them in his hand, he blows on the feathered skirt, and the first of Lola's songs is heard on the soundtrack seconds before we see Lola herself. From then on the two strands intertwined in the overture also intertwine in the film itself.

The prostitute in the doorway

Before coming to Lola's all-important songs, however, we can follow out the strand of more traditional music that tells us something of the professor's state of mind, conscious or unconscious, or gives an inkling of his fate. As he walks through the dark and crooked street that leads to The Blue Angel, in one doorway of which a prostitute waits for customers, the sound of singing drifts in from one of the suspect houses: 'Es war einmal/Ein Liebespaar' – 'There was once a pair of lovers.' In the more usual version of this popular song, the opening stanza reads:

Es was einmal	There was once
Ein treuer Husar,	a faithful hussar,
Der liebt sein Mädel	who loved his sweetheart
Ein ganzes Jahr,	A whole year long.
Ein ganzes Jahr	A whole year
Und noch viel mehr,	And much longer still,
Die Liebe nahm	That love
Kein Ende mehr.	Never ended.

That once again catches up the 'faithfulness' notion of 'Treu und Redlichkeit' in an erotic context, which the substitution of 'a pair of lovers' serves to strengthen – and make more ironic in the context of what happens later in the film.[16] This same song will be movingly sung by Susanne Christian at the end of Kubrick's *Paths of Glory*, where the notion of a *soldier* and his sweetheart is particularly apt.

What the Weintraubs-Syncopators, who provide much incidental music (heard only in snatches as the doors of Lola's dressing room open and close), seem to be playing while the scenery is being changed after Lola's first song is a snatch of traditional song:

O du lieber Augustin,	O dear Augustin,
Alles ist hin!	Everything's lost!
Geld ist weg, Mäd'l ist weg,	Money is gone, girl is gone,
Augustin liegt im Dreck!	Augustin lies in the mire!
O du lieber Augustin,	O dear Augustin,
Alles ist hin.	Everything's lost.

This is inaudible in some copies of the film; but when it is heard, it forecasts all too clearly the fate of a professor who becomes an Auguste and does indeed lose his money and – in the end – his woman.

When the professor wakes up in Lola's bed after having drunk more than he has been used to, he finds himself holding a black doll which, when one of its arms is moved, plays the snatch of a tune from Schubert's *Die schöne Müllerin* (*The Fair Maid of the Mill*). The song in question is significantly entitled 'Wohin?' ('Where to?') and

The black doll

one of its stanzas speaks of nixies singing alluringly within a mill-stream's rushing waters. The itinerant young miller who hears them resists their lure, and goes on his way – the professor, clearly, has not been so strong-minded when faced with the nixie of The Blue Angel.

The idyllic breakfast scene that follows, which seems so comfortably domestic and in this respect so different from the cheerless breakfast in the professor's study (between a grumbling housekeeper and a dead bird), is broken by the town hall clock striking eight and reminding him of his duties; he tries to follow them, with 'Treu und Redlichkeit', but encounters nothing but gleeful mockery and hideous noise from his whole class, and cool dismissal from the headmaster after he has announced that he plans to marry the chanteuse in whom he thinks he has found what he secretly desired.

The wedding banquet scene that follows shows Hollaender at a piano striking up the wedding march from Mendelssohn's *Midsummer Night's Dream* suite, followed by the communal singing of 'Hoch soll'n sie leben!' honouring the newly-weds and wishing them a happy

The class's mockery

life. For that, however, the bridegroom is far too inflexible; and after scenes of physical and mental degeneration he dies quasi-petrified in his old schoolroom to orchestral strains of 'Üb immer Treu und Redlichkeit' and the midnight strokes of the same bell we heard at the beginning.

While the professor's music consists of briefly heard snatches, to which the words have, in many cases, to be supplied by the audience from their own experience, Lola performs hers in full, with professional accompaniment and practised ease; and where his are traditional or derive from respected composers that include Mozart, Schubert, Mendelssohn and Silcher, Lola's are specially composed, for performance in the film, by Hollaender, who can be seen at the piano next to the Weintraubs' oboe-player. They are cabaret songs, what we have heard Hollaender call 'chansons' and 'Schlager', written with the limitations of the young Dietrich's voice constantly in mind. The tessitura is high, even deliberately piping in tone where that is appropriate, with just an occasional descent to a lower register which will become one of the hallmarks of Dietrich's later performances in locales worlds removed from the sordidness of The Blue Angel beer hall and variety stage.

The song Lola sings, with an inimitable Berlin pronunciation, when the professor first bursts into The Blue Angel in pursuit of his errant pupils, ostensibly concerns a pi-a-no-la owned by a smart and modish singer who is the toast of the season, 'der Saisong', in Berlinese, rhyming with the 'Salong' in which that pi-a-no-la stands in for something much more intimate. 'Every man loves me, but I won't let anyone touch my pi-a-no-la'. This leads over into a series of puns, terms applying in different senses to a musical instrument and human bodies: 'I'll bash his *strings* ["Saiten", strings of a musical instrument, a homophone of "Seiten", sides, ribs] and stamp on his *pedal*.'

This first song makes it clear that Lola is neither a conventional vamp nor a victim of a male-dominated society. We are confronted with a well-built young woman who makes use of her natural endowments (including, of course, her voice) and revealing costumes to earn her living; who has a 'Berliner Schnauze', the Berliner's gift of the gab, and an earthy sense of humour; and who knows very well how to keep her distance from those down below who have paid to see and hear her, and who clearly relish her performance. She accepts with good grace the shouted orders for beer and popular foodstuffs that punctuate her turn – it's all part of the game, along with shouts of appreciation and invitation which never induce her to leave the stage and wander among the customers. What in fact Hollaender has here given her to sing is a type of *chanson* well known in the contemporary literary cabaret and based on earlier models: the 'Ichgesang' in which a singer assumes a character that may be poor, low-life, sometimes even criminal, and speaks of that character's mode of life and feelings in the first person singular. Dietrich's sophisticated contemporary Blandine Ebinger,[17] and her more down-to-earth friend Claire Waldoff (from whom the young Dietrich had learned a great deal) had many a song of this kind in their repertoire.

Lola's next song is not her exclusive property – we hear it first from Guste, Kiepert's elderly wife: 'Children, tonight I make my choice: a man, a real man, who still wants to kiss and can do it too – a man, a real man.' She sings it while the tatty scenery is being changed: when the backcloth showing a formal pavilion is in place, the song passes to Lola who performs it in a parody of eighteenth-century costume. It's all part of an enticing performance, which includes the direction of a spotlight into the audience – its beam advances the action by alighting on the professor, who has just stumbled into the hall in pursuit of his errant pupils. As in her first song, so here: Dietrich has a way of pitching her performance between enticement and irony. The humour of her performance lies partly in her Berlinese accentuation ('Männah! Männah!'); in her song's lively foxtrot tune; and in the way the Weintraubs underline her effects instrumentally.

Irony is patent in the way Lola begins her performance. She adopts a piping tone as she tells of spring heralded, not by a romantic nightingale, but by a chirping sparrow. Here a clarinet breaks in with an exaggerated tremolo that makes the audience laugh with – never at! – the singer, who now expresses a generalised erotic feeling. 'I'm in love with a man, but don't yet know who it will be.' Lola is conscious of the power her looks and her performance skills confer on her – the power to choose among the many kinds of men that respond to her. She is, the singer tells us, thoroughly tired of youngsters (one thinks of the schoolboys that hang around her dressing room); the man she chooses need not be either handsome or rich; he should just be *mature*. It is therefore doubly ironic that at this point the professor stumbles into view: a man whom Lola will treat like a little boy, who responds kindly to such treatment, but who, as husband, will sink into depression and anomie and lead her to seek satisfaction elsewhere while still caring enough for him to share her earnings and defend him against the director of her troupe, who resents the professor's patent inability to adapt to showbusiness duties and ethos. Lola is neither vamp nor prostitute, as her next and most famous song will also make clear.

That song, whose melody – no foxtrot, but a slow waltz – had been first heard in the overture, created a new genre, the *Filmchanson* whose popularity was furthered by four media: film, radio, gramophone and live performance by dance bands, with or without a lead singer. The costume and stance in which Dietrich performed it became equally famous and have been endlessly imitated. She wears a top-hat, generally thought of as a masculine head covering: but instead of the usual black hers is white, and the costume, which leaves her arms bare and allows a generous swathe of thigh to be seen between black suspenders, allows no doubt of

her femininity. Beginning in standing position, swaying occasionally and closing her eyes, she eventually sits down on a wooden cask, raising a leg whose knee she clasps with both hands.

The song begins with lines that convey the enigmatic fascination of feminine beauty: 'a mysterious effulgence, a je ne sais quoi, shines from a beautiful woman's eyes'. That introduction leads to the dreamy rendition of a line known in English as 'Falling in love again'. In German it says something rather different: 'Ich bin von Kopf bis Fuss auf Liebe eingestellt' – 'I am geared to (*or* switched on to) love from head to foot'. Like the sparrow rather than the nightingale in the previous song, so this mechanical image pays its tribute to the Neue Sachlichkeit (New Sobriety) movement that had by then succeeded Expressionism in Germany, and to the lyrics of Erich Kästner, which best embodied it in verses that often became cabaret songs. The gesture with which Dietrich accompanies this line, leaning back and sweeping her hand through the air alongside her body from head to foot, is also more meaningfully adapted to the German rather than the English text. That and nothing else, the song proclaims, is Lola's world: 'Ich kann halt Liebe nur, und sonst garnichts.' 'Men,' the song continues, with conventional imagery, 'cluster round me, like moths around a flame, and if it burns them, I am not to blame ...'. We are aware of watching an audience depicted on the screen watching a skilful professional performance; but we must also feel that something of Lola's nature is being revealed here, something which the professor, who watches from a box at the side of the stage with obvious delight, will later come up against to his cost. He is himself being watched at this juncture: Kiepert has drawn the audience's attention to his presence, and Lola is

The professor's delight

clearly conscious of his fascinated glances and delighted body movements.

Hollaender has provided Dietrich with another song, reinforcing Lola's 'keep off' warning in the earlier ditty that introduced her as 'die fesche Lola' – the smart and fetching one.

Nimm dich in acht vor blonden Fraun	Beware of blonde women
Die haben so etwas Gewisses.	They have a certain something.
's is ihnen nicht gleich anzuschaun,	You can't tell at first glance,
Aber irgend etwas iss es!	But there is something!

The elision ''s is' (for 'es ist'), and the rhyme 'Gewisses' / 'iss es' (for 'ist es') belong as surely to Lola's Berlinese persona as the rhyme 'Saisong' / 'Salong', and the pronunciation 'Männah' (for 'Männer', men) in her earlier offerings. We hear Lola singing this off-screen (five years after an unsuitable marriage proposal which she had at first laughed at, but had then been flattered into accepting) while the ex-professor tries to earn a little something by hawking around the postcard images of Lola that had first aroused his latent sexuality. There seems little of the latter left: he has let himself go, is unshaven and carelessly dressed, as he passes along the tables offering his wares to a public he despises as an 'uneducated mob'.

Lola's song-refrain continues:

Ein kleines Blickgeplänkel sei erlaubt dir,	You may safely exchange a few amorous glances,
Doch denke immer: Achtung vor dem Raubtier!	But be ever wary of the feral beast!

That last image takes the audience into the psycho-sexual world of Frank Wedekind, himself an eminent practitioner of the cabaret song, who had introduced *his* Lulu in the guise of a *dompteur* of wild animals, armed with a whip.

It is this very song which Lola sings when, despite the professor's protests, the troupe returns to The Blue Angel, where he is to be exhibited in the guise of a clown before the town in which he had formerly held such a respectable position. Announced by a poster which depicts, not the almost naked woman of the Lola Lola announcement in the tobacconist's window, but a flapper in a 1920s' dance frock, she is now backed, not by the fat beer-swilling apparitions of yore, but by a slimmer troupe of young women who go into a provincial version of a Tiller-girl routine. The unmistakable menace of this song comes from a new Lola, one made harder by her experiences – the imperiously outstretched arm

Lola flanked by flappers

Forcing the wig on the professor

with which she forces her wretched husband to don his clown's wig and get himself onto the stage as Kiepert's Auguste is that of a dominatrix. And when the catastrophe has happened – when her sexual response to Mazeppa, while her husband is being made the butt of Kiepert's physical jokes, has driven the latter into a murderous rage restrained by a straitjacket, from which he is freed only to creep towards his death – it is then that Lola reprises her theme song, proclaiming herself 'geared to love from head to foot'. She sings it, however, in a wholly different way: in a black costume designed by Dietrich herself, wearing what contemporary audiences could recognise as a hat traditionally worn by itinerant (male) cabinet-makers, and a pair of fashionable boots, keeping her arms clutching the back of the chair astride which she sits, or else clasping her hips or resting her hands on her legs. There are no inviting gestures sweeping from head to foot in harmony with her words: her look

Creeping towards death

Lola's reprise

is defiant, imperious, proclaiming her needs with neither flattery nor shame.

And so the strands of the professor's music and Lola's intertwine in double helix fashion, and each ends where it began: Lola's with the *Schlager* melody that the overture announced as her signature tune; the professor's with the traditional tune by which the town hall clock reminds its listeners to be faithful and honest right up to their descent into the coolness of their grave.

Just as the professor's world is full of traditional music, by composers ranging from Mozart to Silcher, so Lola's is full of more ephemeral stuff: the snatches that are heard in Lola's dressing room whenever the door to the stage is opened, or the parody of 'oriental' music to which one of the fat damsels on the stage does a strange, swaying dance while rolling her eyes. The two strands come together when the melody of Schubert's 'Wohin?', which has its relevance to the professor's situation, comes from the black doll on Lola's bed (Dietrich's mascot, by the way, which she smuggled into other films in which she starred); and when Lola accuses her depressed husband that every time she is in a good mood 'markierst du den Bajazzo' – you start impersonating Pagliacci.[18]

One snatch of music heard from The Blue Angel stage is of great historical interest, however: the fragment of a 'couplet' in which a common refrain is used in different senses in successive stanzas. One stanza we hear promises a bright future for a German people that is not divided in itself:

Und die Zukunft leuchtet rings	And the future shines bright
Wenn ihr alle einig seid,	if you are all united:
Vorne, hinten, oben, unten	in front, up high, below,
Rechts und Links.	Right and Left.

This patriotic refrain (coming at the end of a couplet whose earlier stanzas are crudely humorous) is enthusiastically repeated by the assembled eaters and drinkers. Its particular interest lies in its performance by one of the *grandes dames* of the Weimar cabaret, Rosa Valetti, who plays Guste; no phonograph recording of her art has surfaced so far, so that this fragment of a 'couplet', and her hip-thrusting rendition of the song about 'choosing a man' soon to be taken up by Lola, are the only evidence we have of her once so famous style of performance.

Rosa Valetti

Once one has followed out the series of contrasts presented by what we can now call 'the professor's music' and 'Lola's music' one soon becomes aware that more than any other of Sternberg's films *The Blue Angel* is built throughout on contrast and counterpoint. The characters' clothes are an obvious instance: Lola's skimpy costumes with their feathers and frills are opposed to the professor's tight black formal dress which, in its turn, counterpoints that of Kiepert, which seems a caricature of the professor's until the latter has to don the colourful garb of an Auguste, with its enormous loose collar and ever more battered top-hat, presenting a contrast between his former and his present self.

Contrast and counterpoint also appear in the main characters' ages: not only between the professor and his pupils, who resent his authority and shake it off as soon as they spy a chink in his armour, inverting their relation with a cruelty that far outdoes his petty tyrannies, but also in the difference between the visibly ageing professor sinking into anomie, and the still young and vital Lola, who earns a living for them both and protects him from abuse, but whose own needs he cannot, in the end, satisfy.

Sternberg's *mise en scène* structures his film through spatial contrasts too, which resolve themselves into counterpoint between different kinds of order and disorder. The first words spoken in the film are the muttered complaints of the professor's housekeeper about the stacks of books and cigar-ends that clutter his rooms and cause a pestilential fug ('alles verpestet', a significant olfactory suggestion). This contrasts with the painfully symmetrical order of objects on the teacher's desk, and the way his entrance resolves the knot of pupils clustered about Lohmann as he exhibits his saucy postcards into two symmetrical rows with exact spaces between them. That, in its turn, is countered by the picaresque yet functional disorder of Lola's dressing room, a place of work and transformation with its array of cosmetics, plethora of costumes hanging or draped about, and showbusiness posters on every wall.

The main characters' body language is similarly structured. The professor's gait is measured, his gestures – which include repetitive fussing about the contents of his pockets – stiff and compulsive. Psychologically minded critics have seen in this, and in the ceremonial unfolding of a handkerchief that precedes ritual nose-blowing, signs of

The professor's lodging

Lola's dressing room

anal eroticism.[19] Be that as it may – what matters in the present context is how different this is from Lola's unconstrained gait and easy movements that mirror her relaxed attitude to sexuality which propels her, in the end, into the arms of the virile strong man Mazeppa when the professor becomes more her child than her husband.

Significant differences in facial expression, gesture, and body language bespeak contrasts in temperament which also reflect themselves in modes of speech and silence. Lola's easy tone and tempo puncture the professor's pomposity, when he first bursts into her dressing room in search of his straying pupils, as easily as Kiepert's attempts to assert his authority over her. Kiepert's volubility and rapidity of utterance when, on their first encounter, he won't let the professor get a word in edgeways as he crowds him with his large belly, stand out starkly against the silence of the two different kinds of clown who observe the professor's growing fascination with Lola and foreshadow his own ultimate fate, and that of the janitor who lights him on his last way.

Such contrasts as these connect with related contrasts of speech register. The professor's language is formal, bookish – Lola's is more slangy and direct. The marriage proposal is a case in point:

PROF.: Würden Sie dieses als Geschenk von mir annehmen? Und darf ich gleichzeitig um Ihre Hand anhalten?	PROF.: Would you accept this (ring) as a gift from me? And may I simultaneously ask for your hand?
LOLA: Mich willste heiraten?	LOLA: You wanna marry me?

'Willste' for 'willst du?' is Berlinese as opposed to the professor's standard High German; his formal 'Sie' is countered by her familiar 'du'; his old-fashioned conventional 'um Ihre Hand anhalten' is deflated by the everyday simplicity of her 'heiraten', followed by a gust of laughter which the professor characteristically answers with yet another of his old-fashionedly courteous formulae:

Ich hoffe, mein Kind, du bist dir des Ernstes dieser Stunde voll bewusst.	I hope, my child, you are fully conscious of the seriousness of this hour.

Her idiom is also more vivid and picturesque: when she asks her husband to shave in order to improve his ever more neglected appearance, she does so in terms more suitable to the swallowing of medicine:

Du könn'st wirklich mal was zum Rasieren einnehmen!	You could really dose yourself with some shaving-tackle!

Other members of the troupe are also prone to this kind of picturesque catachresis with which Berliners like to spice their remarks. When the professor inadvertently blocks the path of one of the fat ladies of the chorus, she says to him: 'Mensch, Sie sind ja das reinste Verkehrshindernis' – which makes him a traffic jam or traffic bottleneck.

The speech registers of Lola and her professor are not the only ones played against one another in this pioneering sound film. There is also the stage magician's patter designed to veil his sleights of hand from his 'honoured public'; the policeman's periphrastic *Amtsdeutsch*, the bureaucratic speech he has been trained to use ('... dass hier 'ne Körperverletzung begangen worden ist' – 'that grievous bodily harm has been committed here'); and the sea captain's professional speech ('Dreimaster', a ship with three masts) and snatches of English ('der Rowdy'). For much of this Zuckmayer and Liebmann were responsible; but its presence in the film and structural importance is due to Sternberg, whose own German had grown rusty – Vollmöller had served as an interpreter during script conferences – but who, as Marlene Dietrich recalls, took great delight in the picturesque expressions he allowed into his film.[20] The English-speaking version of *The Blue Angel* irons most of this out: but when we hear Lola call the professor her 'Sugardaddy' it throws a bridge across from Berlinese Lola to the feisty heroines of American films played by such stars of the later 1920s and 1930s as Clara Bow, Jean Harlow, and Joan Blondell, and to all the 'Gold-digger' movies that enlivened the Depression.

Here we come to the slyest of the contrasts Sternberg introduced into *The Blue Angel*. He induced Jannings to perform with just the same sort of detail as he had in his silent movies, and made him open and close his first sound film with silent sequences. Except for whistling to his dead bird, the professor does not speak all through breakfast, his fussy preparations for departure, and his leaving by his front door, until he arrives at the school, enters his classroom, and commands his pupils, who have respectfully risen, to sit down with a single word: 'Setzen!' At the end, after the inarticulate crowing cry which forms the climax and catastrophe of *The Blue Angel*, he never speaks any more through all that follows, while Lola reprises her theme song. To drive his point home Sternberg introduces deliberate reminiscences of Jannings's earlier silent films. He loses his position and his class like the general of *The Last Command*, busies himself with a woman's stockings like Huller in *Varieté*, and trudges to oblivion through inhospitable streets like the lost soul of *The Way of All Flesh*.

This association with an art and an acting style now beginning to be old-fashioned is one of the ways through which Sternberg transformed what was conceived as a vehicle for Emil Jannings into a work that celebrated the talent and beauty of Marlene Dietrich. Her earlier films had occasionally shown something of the 'Marlene look' achieved by Sternberg through imaginative lighting, tricks of make-up like the famous stroke of greasepaint along her nose which concealed the *Entennase* (duck-nose) of which she had been painfully conscious in her early years, and the veilings and shadings which became one of this director's trademarks. *Die Frau, nach der man sich sehnt* had captured the look briefly in an image of Dietrich looking out of a train window through the locomotive's steam;[21] but it was left to Sternberg to fashion the icon he began to form in Germany and perfected in Hollywood in six further films with the same fascinating star. Jannings's performance was excellent in its way, both pitiful and terrifying; but it recalled silent performances that had already been caricatured in the mid-1920s, notably by Reinhold Schünzel in Oswald's *Lumpen und Seide* (*Rags and Silk*) of 1924. It also had much in common with performances by other intense actors like Werner Krauss, with whom he had co-starred in Murnau's *Tartüff* in parts that could easily have been interchanged.

Dietrich's performance, on the other hand, struck contemporaries as something new and unique. Louise Brooks had come somewhere near in Pabst's *Pandora's Box*; but Dietrich's Lola is so much more knowing, more deliberately flaunting, and so much more humorous, than Brooks's

The Last Command (left), *Pandora's Box*

assumption of Wedekind's Lulu. Garbo, in her only appearance in a German film, Pabst's *Die freudlose Gasse* (*The Joyless Street*), had been a beautiful frightened doe, in need of being rescued from predators by strong men without any of Lola's fundamental toughness; and such of her Hollywood films as had reached Germany projected her marvellously photogenic beauty with a mysterious remoteness worlds away from Lola's vulgar earthiness. Asta Nielsen was an actress of great intensity, coiled like a spring, with a spare body whose sensuality was almost abstract, who could simulate by sheer force of will youth and age alike, concentrating attention on her expressive face, eyes and hands; she had successfully played Lulu in an earlier film version of Wedekind's play, but Dietrich's cabaret-honed personality was beyond her considerable range. Brigitte Helm's classical profile and youthful body was best employed playing alluring otherworldly beings (*Metropolis*, *Alraune*) or women in other ways removed from the normal commerce of mankind (*Die Liebe der Jeanne Ney*, in which she played a blind girl). For the rest: Pola Negri was the latest and best incarnation of the dark-haired, eye-flashing vamp of non-German appearance – the kind of look against which Lola's song 'Nimm dich in acht vor *blonden* Fraun', and her Berlinese accentuations, insinuatingly polemicised. The blonde woman of German film was the 'motherly Venus' Henny Porten, a slightly podgy amalgam of Gretchen and *Hausfrau*, idolised by many contemporary filmgoers (including the teenage Dietrich herself) as the ideal German star; Dietrich had been made immune to her influence by contacts with the down-to-earth Claire Waldoff and such cabaret stars as the ironic, pencil-thin Margo Lion. The ubiquitous Mia May offered no points of comparison either, beyond her blondeness: she was essentially an action star, rescued from various dilemmas in the films of her husband Joe May; she hardly registered as a strong personality in her own right. Lya de Putti came near Dietrich in sexual charge; but she played too much on one note as an object to be desired and fought over, without the young Dietrich's vitality, warmth, and sense of humour, which she was later to recapture in *Destry Rides Again*. Then there was Ossi Oswalda, a bubbly flapper who fitted perfectly into Lubitsch's early Jewish comedies as a Gentile object of desire and who played a mechanical doll in the same director's *Die Puppe* (*The Doll*) with no trace of Hoffmannesque demonism. Lilian Harvey, with her projection of comradely sweetness lightened by mischievous provocation, had not yet come into her own;

her day would come once she had been teamed with Willy Fritsch as Germany's favourite young couple in operetta films by Thiele, Martin and Charell. And then, of course, audiences had been delighted by the art of the young Elisabeth Bergner, whose spare, androgynous body always seemed driven beyond its strength, kept going by a nervous force that had animated her stage performances as Rosalind in *As You Like It* but which also could break into hysteria, consumed by passions too strong for her, in parts such as *Fräulein Else* in Czinner's film of 1929. This too was as far from Lola as could be imagined.

Even without her songs Dietrich would have struck her first audiences as something quite new in contemporary films; with them, she had taken the first step towards becoming a world star. She had been fortunate to do so under the aegis of a director who had recognised her special qualities and had woven them into that intricate network of contrasts, intertwinings and counterpoint which had made *The Blue Angel* – as Hollaender had recognised – 'tend towards music'.

6

. . . .

'DER BLAUE ENGEL': STERNBERG'S *GERMAN* FILM

In an earlier chapter I tried to show how deliberately Sternberg sought to shut out the actual world by constructing a virtual one that would convey psychological patterns dear to him. In his efforts to show himself sole creator of this world he would occasionally speak, like Shakespeare's Coriolanus, as though he were 'author of himself/And knew no other kin'. Part of the way in which he conveyed this was through a network of recurrent symbolic props: frills, feathers, silk stockings, birds, towering clocks and their bells, grotesque sculptures and caricatures, nets and changing poster designs are some of the most obvious ones. These often refer back to his earlier films (Evelyn Brent's feathers in *Underworld*, the caricatures in the stokers' hold in *The Docks of New York*) or look forward to his later ones (grotesque sculptures in *The Scarlet Empress* – where bells play a terrifying part in a dream sequence – huge, bobbing carnival heads in *The Devil Is a Woman*). In his eagerness to proclaim himself sole begetter of *The Blue Angel*, he even denied the existence of a screenplay, other than his own notes, Liebmann's technical instructions

A gargoyle on the clock

for the benefit of the UFA personnel, and a few suggestions from Zuckmayer – all of which he modified when it came to the actual filming. In his mind, as his autobiography makes clear, the world he created on screen was his own inner one, and owed nothing to actual conditions in Germany (*The Blue Angel*), Russia (*The Scarlet Empress*), China (*Shanghai Express*), or Spain (*The Devil Is a Woman* – a title foisted on him by the studio instead of *Rhapsodie Espagnole*).

Now that Zuckmayer's prose treatment, and the various scenarios scripted by the writing team, are in the public domain, it is possible to see how much of the film is already contained in these; but one also has to appreciate how Sternberg selected from them and gave them a new shape through his mastery of lighting and unerring camera-eye. It is also possible, however, to see these earlier scripts as one of the conduits through which Weimar patterns and concerns seeped into *The Blue Angel* and made it a *German* film; another, of course, being Sternberg's previous study and admiration of the work of star directors of Weimar Germany, and that of their gifted cameramen and designers.

Siegfried Kracauer, who had dismissed *The Blue Angel* in 1930 as too remote from the social world within which it was produced, later came to see in it – as in the work of other film-makers of the 1920s and early 1930s – anticipations of the cruelties and tyrannies of the Nazi régime. The backward teleology of his influential 'psychological history of German film', *From Caligari to Hitler*, which saw everything from the perspective of the Nazi period, has been countered, in recent years, by a forward teleology practised by distinguished critics like Anton Kaes, which has shown how much of these same works was affected by the experiences of army tyrannies in World War I, the loss of that war after supreme efforts, thwarted, it was believed, by a 'stab in the back' by civilians who made peace before the armies had been definitively defeated, by the assignment of 'war guilt' followed by the imposition of heavy 'reparations' payments and the quartering of French and British troops on German soil, and, of course, by the worst monetary inflation in recent history, in which many fortunes were lost while vast sums accrued to *Raffkes*, greedy profiteers. The period had also seen a series of insurrections that were bloodily put down if they came from the left but treated gently when they came from the right. To trace how such things may have seeped into films and produced common themes and atmosphere is a delicate matter; all this concluding chapter can do is to point to a few ways in which, by some sort of osmosis, Weimar Germany might have got into the private world Sternberg sought to construct in *The Blue Angel* as elsewhere.

Take the tragedy of Professor Rath, as he appears in Sternberg rather than Heinrich Mann. Weimar films seem obsessed with disoriented male figures, which may be found at the centre of such disparate works as Joe May's *Das indische Grabmal*, Richard Oswald's *Anders als die Andern* (*Different from the Rest*), *Der ewige Zweifel* (*The Eternal Doubt*), directed by Oswald and scripted by E. A. Dupont, Dupont's own *Varieté*, Pabst's *Geheimnisse einer Seele* (*Secrets of a Soul*), Murnau's *Der letzte Mann*, known in England as *The Last Laugh*. In the last two tragedy is avoided by a sudden twist at the end which convinces nobody and is, indeed, ironised by the only intertitle of Murnau's pioneering film. It is hardly surprising that this disoriented figure, and the sado-masochistic situations in which it is so often involved, should surface so prominently under the conditions of the Weimar Republic; or that so many protagonists, male and female, commit suicide, like poor Mother Krause in Phil Jutzi's ironically titled *Mutter Krausens Fahrt ins Glück* (*Mother Krause's Journey into Happiness*), who takes a child with her on that journey. Professor Rath's end is not exactly a suicide, but he clearly wills his death when he feels that there is nothing more to hope for.

A feeling that the professor of *The Blue Angel* shares with many who lost their fortunes in the great German inflation is that he has been flung out of his own class and made economically dependent on people he feels to be beneath him – 'ungebildetes Pack', an uncultured crew, he calls the customers to whom he tries to flog his saucy postcards, only to be reminded that Lola earns a living from them for him as well as herself.

The most obvious parallel is Councillor Rumfort in Pabst's inflation-film *Die freudlose Gasse*, but German and Austrian films are filled with other equally resentful figures. The obverse of such despair is a hunger for entertainment, often with sexual titillation, provided by the false Maria's dance in Lang's *Metropolis*; or Anita Berber's turn (cut down by the Weimar censors) in the same director's first film featuring Dr Mabuse; and, of course, by Kiepert's variety troupe and its provocative star in *The Blue Angel*.

That disorientation, loss of status and feelings of inadequacy may lead to sexual malfunction is a frequent theme of the 'Enlightenment Films' (Aufklärungsfilme) that proliferated in the early years of the Republic and found its Freudian expression in the already mentioned *Secrets of a Soul*. After his brief attraction and excitement by Lola the professor soon sinks into a depression that makes him an inadequate sexual partner who drives Lola into the arms of a more potent male. He is a sad failure as a husband as well as a clown.

Another facet of his disorientation is his changed relation to time. At the beginning we see him routinely ordering his life by the town hall clock and its chimes, by the clock over the school's entrance surmounted by the motto 'Ora et labora', summoning to prayer and to daily labour, and by his own pocket-watch, panickily consulted at Lola's breakfast table. After his dismissal he finds it impossible to adjust to a world that regulates itself, not by public clock time, but by bells that shrill in dressing rooms to summon its denizens, at varying intervals, to take their turns on the stage. There is order here too, and obligation to do one's duty, but he finds these duties repellent and their summons too contrary to the routines his many years as a schoolmaster have accustomed him to. In his excellent book *Cinema and Society* Paul Monaco has traced the use of the clock as a *leitmotif* in a number of German films of the 1920s, from Dieterle's *Geschlecht in Fesseln* (*Sex in Chains*) to *Mutter Krausens Fahrt ins Glück*, pertinently commenting that in these German films the clock usually represented impending danger or disaster rather than just the passing of time. How this fits Professor Rath, once his infatuation with Lola has shaken him out of his accustomed routine, needs no further analysis.

Sternberg's acceptance of the UFALAND constructed for him by Hunte and Hasler points to another parallel with Weimar films from *Caligari* onwards. These constructions recall an idyllic small-town world, like that seen in the Biedermeier townscapes of Karl Spitzweg (1808–83); but the idyll is invaded and disrupted by itinerant strangers who transform idyll into nightmare. Caligari penetrates Holstenwall with his murderous somnambulist (though this may be part of Francis's sick imagination), Kiepert's troupe, with its fascinating star, penetrates a small harbour town and unleashes pandemonium in the professor's schoolroom and disrupts his previously secure existence. Fear of destructive outsiders evoked echoes in the mind of many respectable citizens of the Weimar Republic, who endured foreign occupations and had uneasy feelings that people regarded as outsiders occupied prominent positions in the cultural and commercial life of their state. That the sneakiest of the schoolboys, called Kieselack in Mann's novel, should have been renamed 'Goldstaub' as early as Zuckmayer's prose adaptation, where he is overtly said to be Jewish, adds an ominous note to this theme.

The spectacle of a clash of generations is one presented in many Weimar films – the title of one of these, *Jugendtragödie* may stand for most of them. In the context of Weimar Germany this theme, already common to novels, plays and films of the Wilhelmine Empire, has a special twist: the generation that lost the war, allegedly 'stabbed in the back' by its contemporaries at home, now wielded an authority that was felt to be oppressive. Professor Rath, seen by his boys as a tyrant and slave-driver, unleashes a schoolroom rebellion that seeks to wound him cruelly as soon as a chink appears in his armour. The early scenarios of *The Blue Angel* had contained a passing reference to the Spartakus rebellions in the Berlin of 1918, a communist revolt soon repressed by the Social Democrat authorities. Sternberg deleted that, along with other allusions to what was going on outside the studio walls of Babelsberg; but the rebellion in the professor's classroom, soon crushed by the headmaster who, however, also has the professor dismissed, may be seen as paralleling other rebellions from the right as well as the left. Kracauer came to think of the instigators of that classroom *putsch* as ideal material for the Hitler Youth.

Another feeling aroused by Sternberg's choice of setting and his *mise en scène* is one of claustrophobia. The only glimpse of sky we see is either grey and obscured by smoke, or glimpsed through a dim skylight in the professor's bedroom, which is as cluttered with books as his desk and his breakfast table. Double framing by black stove-pipes running

The professor's skylight

Otto Hunte's sketch for the street
leading to The Blue Angel
(Filmmuseum Berlin)

Sternberg eliminated both ship
and sky

across a room, mirrors that multiply the characters' image and doubly shut them in, folding screen, nets, anchors hanging from ceilings, scenery behind a cramped and crowded stage, all reinforce a claustrophobic feeling that *The Blue Angel* shares with such works as Leopold Jessner's *Hintertreppe – Ein Film-Kammerspiel (Backstairs – a Filmed Chamber-Play)*. In other German films of the time the feeling of occlusion, natural to a people that has lost its overseas colonies and experienced foreign occupation of the Rhineland and Saar provinces, was apt to take two contrasting forms: a fear of the streets outside the home, an outside where danger lurked but which offered a promise of adventure that turned out to be so perilous that the protagonist flees back to the sheltering home, where a dull wife offers a motherly bosom and a terrine of soup (Grune's *Die Strasse / The Street*); or compensatory flights into imagined exotic lands, like Joe May's popular serial *Die Herrin der Welt* (*Mistress of the World*) and the already mentioned *Indian Tomb*. The return home which appears as rescue to the protagonist of *The Street* is, for Professor Rath, the ultimate nightmare in which he is brought back to the town from which he had started out to be humiliated before the assembled townsfolk and cuckolded by his wife.

But of course, what is best-remembered, worldwide, is not the professor's tragedy, but Lola's triumph. Her songs breathe the security and self-acceptance her husband lacks. She knows that she lives in a world of commercial exchange, and that her young body, and the artistry of her singing, have an exchange value that earns her the admiration of men (even Kiepert, who has felt the sharp edge of her Berlinese tongue often enough, calls her a 'fabelhaftes Weib' – a 'fabulous woman') and makes her a role model for women like the window-washer at the opening of the film, who admires the sexual freedom suggested by the provocative poster to which Sternberg's camera so often returns. Whether she will eventually dwindle into the likeness of Guste, for whom, as Kiepert says, nobody would dream of buying champagne, remains an open question in a film whose last word is 'garnichts', nothing. But we have seen her asserting her sexuality and hardening under her experiences, and can vicariously share her triumph as she sits astride her chair listening to the acclamations of the inner-diegetic audience of whose approval she is sure.

As well she might be – for we know that what they, in fact, have been hearing and seeing, is not Lola, but Marlene Dietrich. The irony with which she performs, the fact that with her tatty costumes she wears what contemporaries recognised as shoes and boots from her own special last in the workshop of Berlin's most fashionable shoemaker, the presence, on the tawdry stage, of Hollaender, Valetti and Gerron (who had so often provided Berlin's most sophisticated entertainments), along with a fashionable contemporary jazz group – all this took contemporary audiences well beyond The Blue Angel into one of the centres of the Weimar Republic's cultural life. Later audiences can catch a reflection of that, enriched by memories of Sternberg's other films (six of the most distinguished with the same female star) and of Dietrich's unique contribution to the art of the cabaret. None of this is necessary, however, for an appreciation of *The Blue Angel* – the still fascinating product of an American director's collaboration with the wealth of talent UFA put at his disposal in the dying days of the Weimar Republic.

EPILOGUE

The Blue Angel is one of a group which the film historian Jerzy Toeplitz has called the 'sign-post films' of a new era that brought film nearer to the Wagnerian *Gesamtkunstwerk* by adding significant acoustic experiences in the outside world as well as sounds that mirrored psychic sensations. The mournful sirens that accompany the professor's last walk speak of the harbour and the sea that we are never shown in Sternberg's deliberately closed off, claustrophobic *Kammerspiel* world, but they also contribute to the evocation of a mood, and deepen the silence surrounding them. In ways already examined Sternberg and Hollaender between them used music for structural purposes that assimilated the whole film to the condition of music in ways which recalled Wagner's interplay of *leitmotifs* that speak of character and fate. For Toeplitz, Sternberg's film therefore holds an honoured place among other sign-post films like Vidor's *Hallelujah* and Mamoulian's *Applause*, Dupont's *Atlantic* and Hitchcock's *Blackmail*, Clair's *Sous les Toits de Paris*, and Genina's *Prix de Beauté*.[22]

At its first performance the film was rapturously received, and it proved popular with later visitors to the Berlin Gloria-Palast of the première, and to less palatial cinemas all over Germany. The critics too found much to praise, particularly in Dietrich's performance; but there were dissentient voices. These came from admirers of Heinrich Mann's social satire on the left of the political spectrum, and from Hugenberg's allies on the right – particularly the ever more vocal National Socialists, with whom several members of the UFA control board more or less openly sympathised. The Hugenberg press tried to minimise the damage by claiming, shortly before the film's opening on 1 April 1930, that *The Blue Angel* was a film *against* Heinrich Mann – but Mann himself loyally declared that he was wholly satisfied with the changes that he had, indeed, approved beforehand, and Pommer seconded him by substituting '*with*' for '*against*'.[23] Critics on the left, however, felt that 'against' was correct: that far too many concessions had been made to Hugenberg and his cohorts and had converted an intellectually powerful and socially explosive novel into what the critic of the respected journal *Weltbühne* called 'ein larmoyantes, unintelligentes Spiesserstück' – a 'tearjerking, unintelligent piece of philistinism'. Theodor Adorno would endorse that judgment some twenty years later.[24]

Nor was the extreme nationalist and the Nazi press mollified by Hugenberg's manoeuvres. Goebbels's *Völkischer Beobachter*, which had regularly censured Hugenberg for his employment of Jews, saw in *The Blue Angel* 'Jewish erotic thinking … What is at work here is a Jewish attempt to subvert and besmirch the German character and German educational values; here Jewish cynicism shows itself with a baseness that is seldom seen so openly.'[25] Six years later, after Hitler and his party were securely in power, another critic attacked the film from another side. For him the film went counter to the spirit of the new age because it was unheroic; that instead of being fired by hatred and *Schadenfreude* to wreak revenge on the society that had sought to cast him out, like Mann's Professor Unrat, the professor of Sternberg's film was a weakling who allowed himself to be victimised without fighting back with anything but a last despairing outbreak that landed him in a straitjacket.[26]

When that critique was penned, in 1936, *The Blue Angel* had disappeared from German screens, and was not shown again publicly until the Nazi régime had collapsed amid the ruins of Berlin. What happened to those who had worked on Sternberg's and Pommer's film makes an instructive footnote to twentieth-century history; but in the restricted compass of this book it can only be roughly sketched in.

Of Dietrich little need be said. Her place is secure in the history of film and cabaret; many books have been written in appreciation of her art, and the ups and downs of her life have been chronicled *ad infinitum*. She was abused in postwar Germany by many who could not forgive her for donning American uniform and entertaining American troops when the US was at war with Germany; many more, however, commended her resolute anti-Nazi stance and her refusal of all blandishments by Goebbels and others to return to Nazi Germany. Her mentor Sternberg made six more films with her in the US, classics one and all; he continued directing, often under adverse conditions, after their partnership ended, but never made another film in Germany.

Friedrich Hollaender left Germany immediately after the Nazi takeover; he reached the US via Paris in 1933, tried at first to continue his cabaret career there but soon found his feet in Hollywood where, as Frederick Hollander, he supplied a multitude of compositions, from whole musical continuities to single songs – some of the latter for Dietrich in films like *Seven Sinners* and *A Foreign Affair* – to major studios: Paramount, Warner Bros. and Universal. Franz Wachsmann, who orchestrated the *Blue Angel* songs, also became a much sought-after composer in Hollywood, and died in Los Angeles in 1967. Most of the core members of the Weintraubs-Syncopators escaped from Nazi persecution to Australia.

Pommer and Zuckmayer worked on English films for a while, the former for the Mayflower company he had founded with Charles Laughton, the latter with Korda. Both eventually emigrated to the US, where Pommer worked for a while in the production department of RKO until a severe illness interrupted him. He recovered sufficiently to return to Germany after World War II, realising several projects with Intercontinental Film before returning to Los Angeles, where he died in 1966. Zuckmayer reached the US in 1939, deprived of his German citizenship; he worked briefly in the Warner Bros.' script department but left to continue writing while farming in Vermont. His play *Des Teufels General* (*The Devil's General*), written in 1942, became one of postwar Germany's greatest theatrical successes and was filmed in 1954–5. He became a Swiss citizen and settled in Switzerland but collaborated on the scripts of several postwar films. He died in Switzerland in 1977. Vollmöller also found the atmosphere of Hitler's Germany uncongenial; he travelled widely, often flying his own aeroplane, and settled, ultimately, in the US. He served as one of the scriptwriters on Sternberg's *The Shanghai Gesture* and died in Los Angeles seven years later. Heinrich Mann emigrated to France in 1933 and reached the US via Spain in 1940.

He tried, unsuccessfully, to break into film authorship in Hollywood, but continued to write novels (two of which have been filmed) until his death in 1950 as he was preparing to take up a post as president of the newly founded Academy of Arts in the German Democratic Republic.

Two of the boys were also lost to German films. Robert Klein-Lörk emigrated to the US and vanished from public view until he died in New York in 1963. The Dutch-born Rolant (later Roland) Varno, who had already had experience in Hollywood films in 1932, had parts in two Dutch films in 1934, and then migrated back to Hollywood, acting in a number of anti-Nazi films that included *Underground* and *Hostages*, where he co-starred with Luise Rainer. His name also appears lower down the cast list in Reinhold Schünzel's Hollywood film, *Balalaika*.

Karl Huszar-Puffy resumed his Hungarian name Huszár Pufi Karoly when he returned to Hungary in the 1930s. From there he tried to reach the US in 1941 (as Charles Puffy he had had a brief Hollywood career in the 1920s); but he was arrested in Russia and is reported to have died in internment in Kazakhstan in 1943. Robert Liebmann, dismissed by UFA in 1933, is last known to have gone to Paris, where he worked on scripts for a number of (mainly émigré) directors and producers. What happened to him after 1938 I have not, as yet, been able to discover; I have found no record of further contributions he may have made to the art of the cinema.

Most of the other participants in filming *The Blue Angel* continued their careers more or less undisturbed in the new Germany, where two of the principals had a spectacular future. Emil Jannings rose to be one of the most highly honoured actors in the new state, giving distinguished performances in films many of which had more or less obtrusive propaganda intent even when they were adapted from pre-Nazi plays like *Traumulus* or *Der Herrscher* (*The Commander*, from the play *Vor Sonnenuntergang* by Gerhart Hauptmann). One of his finest performances is to be found in the rabidly anti-British, pro-Boer *Ohm Kruger*. 'De-Nazified' after the war, he began filming again in January 1945, but illness intervened and he died in 1950, without having made any more films.

Hans Albers was rather less welcome to the Nazi bosses than Jannings; but his presence was indispensable in German films, in which he conquered his public with irresistible demonstrations of dash, verve, popular speech (with homely Hamburg notes) and a lively way with songs that frequently had a seafaring background. Often presented as a blond 'leader' figure in the Nazi era, he became an excellent character actor after the war, and died in Munich in 1960.

Among those involved in *The Blue Angel*, Kurt Gerron had the saddest fate. Thrown off the film he was busy directing in 1933, he emigrated first to Paris, then to Austria, then to Holland, where he found brief employment in the Dutch film industry and with a Jewish theatre group. Arrested by the Germans in Amsterdam in 1943, he was transported first to the Westerbork and then to the Theresienstadt Concentration Camp. In the latter the Nazi commandant induced him to make a deceptively staged documentary, purporting to show that Jews were well treated there (known as *Der Führer schenkt den Juden einer Stadt/ The Führer Makes the Jews the Present of a City*). As soon as this was completed and shown to the Red Cross and gullible foreigners, the amenities provided as stage dressing (to hide the true conditions in Theresienstadt) were withdrawn, and Gerron, together with others who had worked on the film, was transported to Auschwitz where they were murdered. His memory lives on in *The Blue Angel* and the many other German films in which his gift for (often comic) characterisation can still be seen and admired.

APPENDIX:
A NOTE ON THE ENGLISH VERSIONS
. . . .

Sternberg shot each sequence of *Der Blaue Engel/ The Blue Angel* first in German, then in English, crediting the translation of the dialogue to himself and his assistant Carl Winston, whose brother Sam had acted as assistant director and was entrusted with the preparation of the English version's final cut after Sternberg had left for the US. The cast remained the same in both versions, speaking in passable English some of the time, in German at other times, and occasionally keeping silent where the German version had dialogue. The Winston version was partly recut when Paramount released the film under its own copyright, unveiling it to the New York public on 5 December 1930. This showing at the New York Rialto had been preceded by a London trade show on 3 July and by a first performance at the London Regal on 2 August 1930. The film has since circulated in several versions; the textual situation remains confused, and Sternberg himself, when he referred to film, always spoke of the German version, which alone had his full editorial imprint.

In a widely circulated Paramount print which is in my possession, the film mutilates the symphonic opening over the credits, with dire consequence for the musical structure devised by Sternberg and Hollaender; curtails the dialogue between the professor and his headmaster, which makes the latter's action far more arbitrary than it is; and omits the arrival of Kiepert's reconstituted troupe at The Blue Angel, so that we never see the first erotic sparks flying from Mazeppa to Lola. Other prints have yet other changes (including, in one case, the transfer of Lola's reprise of her theme song to the very end of the film); and I therefore decided, in this short book, to concentrate on the German version, which has remained relatively unaltered since its first release in this country, and is now available in copies subtitled in English.

This is not to say, however, that the English versions are of no interest, as Peter Baxter has pointed out, when he reviewed in *Sight and Sound* a DVD which contains a truncated English version as well as a full-length German one. He compared the former with a longer English print (held in the British Film Institute) which 'closely mirrors the German version in content and structure':

the two English versions contain whole sequences constructed from takes different from one another and different from those in the German film …

A case in point is the sequence where Professor Rath watches Lola Lola sing 'Ich bin von Kopf bis Fuss'/'Falling in Love Again'. In each version the scene fades out on a close-up of the entranced professor. In *Der Blaue Engel* Jannings signals Rath's unanticipated pleasure by coyly shielding the side of his face with his right hand, as if too embarrassed to show his enjoyment. In the print of *The Blue Angel* on the DVD he tugs at his collar with a finger, as if watching Lola makes it difficult for him to breathe. In the *bfi* print the scene ends with Rath delightedly clapping in open, childlike joy.[27]

Other points of interest are shots of Ertzum leading the rebellious class in a mocking song before pandemonium breaks out, and culturally significant variations such as the class being made to write out the word 'the' two hundred times instead of being asked to answer a trick question on *Julius Caesar* when they had prepared *Hamlet*. Some copies also contain outtakes that would fit well into the German version: notably a wordless sequence showing different reactions among members of Lola's public who are offered revealing photos of her by the ex-professor – an opportunity for Sternberg to introduce some more of his German fatties.

Unlike some later examples of multi-language films distributed by UFA, the English versions of *The Blue Angel* use the same actors as the German one throughout. They attempt to justify these actors' obviously foreign accents by making Jannings a professor of English who uses the direct method in his classes, and Dietrich a non-German artist with whom all conversations have to be conducted in English. Among themselves the other characters use a small selection of the original German dialogue. This convention breaks down in the final sequence, in which Kiepert is made to address the German audience that has come to gape at the ex-professor in an English that many of its members could hardly have understood.

Co-operation between the Friedrich Wilhelm Murnau Stiftung, the Filmmuseum Berlin, the Universum Film GMBH and Transit Film of Munich has produced an excellent double DVD which contains, besides useful features such as biographies, portrait photos, screentests, trailers of the 1930s and 1960s, and a chronicle of the film's gestation, digitally remastered copies of the best available German and English versions of *The Blue Angel*. This will allow detailed comparisons not attempted in the present book, whose author remains convinced of the superiority of the German version of Sternberg's classic film over even the best edited English one.

NOTES

· ·

Where publication details are not given, see Select Bibliography

1 Heinrich Mann, *Ausgewählte Werke in Einzelausgaben*, vol. 7 (1954), pp. 122f.
2 John Gage, 'Mood Indigo', *The Romantic Spirit in German Art 1790–1990*, ed. by Keith Hartley et al. (Edinburgh: Scottish National Gallery/London: Hayward Gallery, 1990), p. 122.
3 *Rororo Taschenbuch*, Rowohlt, Hamburg, 1951.
4 'Marlene, Deutschlands ungeliebter Engel', title-page of *Der Spiegel* no. 25, 2000.
5 Luise Discherl and G. Nickel (eds), *Der blaue Engel. Die Drehbuchentwürfe*, pp. 511–12.
6 Maria Riva, *Marlene Dietrich. By Her Daughter*, pp. 63–4.
7 Josef von Sternberg, *Fun in a Chinese Laundry*, p. 125.
8 Marlene Dietrich, *Nehmt nur mein Leben ...*, p. 72.
9 For the context of this see Hans Wisskirchen (ed.), *Mein Kopf und die Beine von Marlene Dietrich*, pp. 6–10.
10 Sternberg, *Fun in a Chinese Laundry*, pp. 228–9.
11 Ibid., pp. 136–7.
12 Jannings discusses this in an interview reported in *Reichsfilmblatt*, 28 March 1930 – see Werner Sudendorf (ed.), *Marlene Dietrich*, p. 108.
13 Sternberg, *Fun in a Chinese Laundry*, p. 138 and passim.
14 *The Blue Angel. An Authorized Translation of the German Continuity*, p. 10.
15 Sudendorf (ed.), *Marlene Dietrich*, pp. 107–8.
16 Discherl and Nickel have useful notes on the provenance of this and other traditional songs. They do not, however, give the popular reading 'ein *treuer* Husar' which had superseded the older 'ein *roter* Husar' by the 1920s.
17 Ebinger was Hollaender's wife; he wrote a group of songs for her in which she impersonated young girls from a poor or even criminal background.
18 The reference is clearly to the sad clown of Leoncavallo's opera rather than the Thomas Mann *Novelle* cited by Discherl and Nickel, which Lola is hardly likely to have read.
19 See Norman O. Brown, 'The Excremental Vision', in *Life against Death. The Psychoanalytic Meaning of History* (Middletown, CT: Wesleyan University Press), pp. 179ff.
20 Dietrich, *Nehmt nur mein Leben ...*, p. 73.
21 See Bach, *Marlene Dietrich*, fourth illustration from the end of the unnumbered photo pages between pp. 130 and 131.
22 Jerzy Toeplitz, *Geschichte des Films*, vol. 2, p. 86.
23 Documents reprinted in Sudendorf (ed.), *Marlene Dietrich*, pp. 111–16.
24 Ibid., pp. 128–30 (Celsius was Carl von Ossietzki) and Wisskirchen (ed.), *Mein Kopf*, p. 82 (Adorno).
25 *UFA Magazin VIII*, p. 7.
26 Richard Bie, *Emil Jannings*, p. 57.
27 See Peter Baxter, 'Fallen Angels', p. 65. In the same review Baxter makes the point that while the film is *visually* artificial, its *aural* features – the noises of the street market, of bar-room crowds and so on – are 'arrestingly realistic, often symbolic, and sometimes maddeningly disorienting'. Some of this disorientation results, I think, from the fact that while such noises are indeed realistic when taken by themselves, their distribution is not. There is no dressing room in the world situated like Lola's between a noisy stage, a busy corridor, and another dressing room housing a miscellaneous group chattering or being shouted at by their director, in which all extraneous sounds cease as suddenly and as totally as they do here when a door is shut. Baxter's point about the symbolic effects of some of the sounds Sternberg introduces is well taken: not only because of those mournful sirens, but also because raucous sounds erupt into Lola's dressing room just at the points where the spectacle she presents to the professor's fascinated gaze ratchets his erotic fascination up another notch.

CREDITS

....

Der Blaue Engel

Germany
1929-30
Release Date
1 April 1930
Production Company
UFA, Berlin: Erich Pommer,
Production Unit
Producer
Erich Pommer
Director
Josef von Sternberg
Writers
Carl Zuckmayer
Karl Vollmöller
adapting the book *Professor
Unrat* by Heinrich Mann in
consultation with the author
and Josef von Sternberg
Screenplay
Robert Liebmann
Music
Friedrich Hollaender
Weintraubs-Syncopators
Orchestrations by Franz
Wachsmann
Song Texts
Friedrich Hollaender
Robert Liebmann
Camera
Günther Rittau
Hans Schneeberger
Set Design
Otto Hunte
Emil Hasler
Sound
Fritz Thiery, recording on
AFIFA Klangfilm apparatus,
assisted by Herbert Kiehl
Costumes
Tihamer Várady
Karl-Ludwig Holub
Make-up
Waldemar Jabs
Oskar Schmidt
Assistant Editor
Sam Winston
Stills
Karl Beyer
Laszlo Willinger

Cast
Emil Jannings
Professor Immanuel Rath
Marlene Dietrich
Lola Lola
Kurt Gerron
Kiepert, Stage Magician
Rosa Valetti
Guste, his wife
Hans Albers
Mazeppa
Reinhold Bernt
A clown
Eduard von Winterstein
Headmaster
Hans Roth
School Janitor (caretaker)
Rolf Müller
Angst
Rolant Varno
Lohmann
Karl Balhaus
Ertzum
Robert Klein-Lörk
Goldstaub
Karl Huszar-Puffy
Landlord of The Blue Angel
Wilhelm Diegelmann
Sea captain
Gerhart Bienert
Policeman
Ilse Fürstenberg
Rath's housekeeper
Friedrich Hollaender
Pianist
Musicians
Weintraubs-Syncopators

Filmed in UFA Studios,
Neubabelsberg, from 4
November 1929 to 22
January 1930

First shown in Gloria-Palast,
Berlin, 1 April 1930

Censorship: 15 March 1930

Trailer: Censorship 29
March 1930: 201m

Black & White
2,965 metres
108 minutes

SELECT BIBLIOGRAPHY

Adorno, Theodor, 'Warum nicht "Professor Unrat"?', *Die neue Zeitung* (Munich), 25 January 1952.

Bach, Steven, *Marlene Dietrich. Life and Legend* (London: HarperCollins, 1992).

Baxter, John, *The Cinema of Josef von Sternberg* (London: Zwemmer, 1971).

Baxter, Peter, *Just Watch! Sternberg, Paramount and America* (London: British Film Institute, 1993).

—— (ed.), *Sternberg* (London: British Film Institute, 1980).

——, 'Fallen Angels', *Sight and Sound* vol. 11 no. 11, November 2001.

Bemmann, Helga, *Marlene Dietrich. Ihr Weg zum Chanson* (Berlin: Musikverlag, 1990).

Bie, Richard, *Emil Jannings: Eine Diagnose des Deutschen Films* (Berlin: Frundsberg, 1936).

The Blue Angel. An Authorized Translation of the German Continuity, with an Introduction by Josef von Sternberg (London: Lorrimer, 1968).

Blumenberg, H.C., *In meinem Herzen ... Hans Albers* (Frankfurt am Main: Fischer Taschenbuch, 1991).

Bock, H.-M. (ed.), *CineGraph. Lexikon zum deutschsprachigen Film* (Munich: edition text + kritik), 1984–2002 (ongoing).

—— and Michael Töteberg (eds), *Das Ufa-Buch: Kunst und Krisen, Stars und Regisseure, Wirtschaft und Politik* (Frankfurt am Main: Zweitausendeins, 1992).

Bowman, Barbara, *Master Space. Film Images of Capra, Lubitsch, Sternberg and Wyler* (New York: Greenwood Press, 1992).

Brownlow, Kevin, *The Parade's Gone By* (London: Secker and Warburg, 1968).

Del Gaudio, Sybil, *Dressing the Part. Sternberg, Dietrich and Costume* (Cranbury, NJ: Associated Presses, 1993).

Dickens, Homer, and J. Vermilye, *The Complete Films of Marlene Dietrich* (New York: Carol, 1992).

Dietrich, Marlene, *Nehmt nur mein Leben ... Reflexionen* (Munich: Bertelsmann, 1979).

Discherl, Luise, and G. Nickel (eds), *Der blaue Engel. Die Drehbuchentwürfe*. Mit einer Chronik von Werner Sudendorf, Zuckmayer–Schriften vol. 4 (St Ingbert: Röhrig Universitätsverlag, 2000).

Elsaesser, Thomas, 'Germany: The Weimar Years', in *The Oxford History of World Cinema*, ed. by G. Nowell-Smith (New York: Oxford University Press, 1996).

Felsmann, Barbara, and K. Prünn, *Kurt Gerron – Gefeuert und gejagt, 1897–1944. Das Schicksal eines deutschen Unterhaltungskünstlers* (Berlin, 1992).

Hagener, Malte, and J. Hans (eds), *Als die Filme singen lernten. Innovation und Tradition im Musikfilm 1928–1983* (Munich: edition text + kritik, 1999).

Hogue, Peter, 'True Blue', *Film Comment* vol. 30 no. 2, March–April 1994.

Holba, Herbert, *Emil Jannings* (Neu Ulm: Knorr, 1979).

Kaes, Anton, 'Film in der Weimarer Republik', in *Geschichte des deutschen Films*, ed. by W. Jacobsen, A. Kaes and H.M. Prinzler (Stuttgart: Metzler, 1993).

Kanzog, Klaus, 'Missbrauchter Heinrich Mann? Bemerkungen zu *Der Blaue Engel*', *Heinrich Mann Jahrbuch* vol. 14, 1996.

Koch, Gertrud, 'Between Two Worlds. Sternberg's Der Blaue Engel', in *German Film and Literature. Adaptations and Transformations*, ed. by E. Rentschler (London: Methuen, 1986).

Koebner, Thomas (ed.), *Idole des deutschen Films* (Munich: edition text + kritik, 1997).

Kracauer, Siegfried, *From Caligari to Hitler. A Psychological History of German Film* (London: Dennis Dobson, 1947).

Kreimeier, Klaus, *Die Ufa-Story, Geschichte eines Filmkonzerns* (Munich: Hanser, 1992).

Mann, Heinrich, *Professor Unrat oder das Ende eines Tyrannen* (Munich, 1905; Berlin: Ullstein, 1925).

——, *Ausgewählte Werke in Einzelausgaben* (Berlin: Aufbau Verlag, 1951–62).

Merigeau, Pascal, *Josef von Sternberg* (Paris: Edilig, 1983).

Monaco, Paul, *Cinema and Society: France and Germany during the Twenties* (New York: Elsevier, 1976).

Mulvey, Laura, 'Visual Pleasure and Narrative Cinema', in *Movies and Methods*, vol. 2, ed. by B. Nichols (Berkeley: University of California Press, 1985).

Naudet, Jean-Jacques, M. Riva, and W. Sudendorf, *Marlene Dietrich. Photographs and Memories* (London: Thames and Hudson, 2001).

O'Connor, Patrick, *The Amazing Blonde Woman. Dietrich's Own Style* (London: Bloomsbury, 1991).

Oms, Marcel, *Josef von Sternberg, 1894–1969* (Paris: Anthologie du Cinéma, 1970).

Patalas, Enno, *Stars – Geschichte der Filmidole* (Frankfurt am Main, Hamburg: Fischer–Bücherei, 1967).

Riva, Maria, *Marlene Dietrich. By Her Daughter* (London: Bloomsbury, 1992).

Sarris, Andrew, *The Films of Josef von Sternberg* (New York: Doubleday, 1966).

Schebera, Jürgen, *Damals in Neubabelsberg. Studios, Stars and Kinopaläste im Berlin der zwanziger Jahre* (Leipzig: Edition Leipzig, 1990).

Schmidt, Eckhart, '*Der blaue Engel.* Protokoll', *Film* vol. 1, 1965, 47–60.

Seesslen, Georg, 'Der blaue Engel. Das exotische Melodram', in *Literaturverfilmung*, ed. by W. Gast (Bamberg: Buchner, 1993).

——, *Erotik. Asthetik des erotischen Kinos*, rev. edn. (Marburg: Schüren, 1996).

Seydel, Renate, and B. Meier, *Marlene Dietrich. Ein Leben in Bildern* (Berlin: Henschel, 2000).

Spiess, Eberhard, *Hans Albers. Eine Filmographie* (Frankfurt am Main: Kommunales Kino, 1997).

Sternberg, Josef von, *Fun in a Chinese Laundry* (San Francisco, CA: Mercury House, 1965).

——, 'The von Sternberg Principle', *Esquire* vol. 60, October 1983.

Studlar, Gaylyn, *In the Realm of Pleasure. Von Sternberg, Dietrich, and the Masochistic Aesthetic* (Urbana: University of Illinois Press, 1988).

Sudendorf, Werner, 'Üb immer Treu und Redlichkeit. Zum *Blauen Engel* von Josef von Sternberg', in S. Wehnet and N. Bielfeldt (eds), *Mein Kopf und die Beine von Marlene Dietrich. Heinrich Manns 'Professor Unrat' und 'Der blaue Engel'* (Lübeck: Buddenbrookhaus, 1996).

—— (ed.), *Marlene Dietrich. Dokumente / Essays / Filme*, vol. 1 (Munich: Hanser, 1977).

——, *Marlene Dietrich* (Munich: Deutscher Taschenbuch Verlag, 2001).

Toeplitz, Jerzy, *Geschichte des Films*, vol. 2: 1928–1933 (Berlin: Henschel, 1985).

UFA Magazin VIII: Die Ufa, das deutsche Bildungsimperium, Eine Ausstellung des Deutschen Historischen Museums und der Stiftung Deutsche Kinemathek (Berlin: Deutsches Historiches Museum, 1992).

Uhlenbrok, Katja, *Musik Spektakel Film. Musiktheater und Tanzkultur im deutschen Film 1922–1947* (Munich: edition text + kritik, 1998).

Wegner, Hart (ed.), *Der Blaue Engel* (New York: Harcourt Brace Jovanovich, 1982).

Weisstein, Ulrich, 'Professor Unrat, Small Town Tyrant, and The Blue Angel: Translations, Versions and Adaptations of Heinrich Mann's Novel in Two Media', in *Proceedings of the 6th Congress of the International Comparative Literature Association* (Stuttgart: Kunst und Wissen [Erich Bieber], 1975).

Wisskirchen, Hans (ed.), *Mein Kopf und die Beine von Marlene Dietrich. Heinrich Manns Professor Unrat und Der Blaue Engel* (Lübeck: Verlag Drägerdruck, 1996).

ALSO PUBLISHED

If you would like further information about future BFI Film Classics or about other books on film, media and popular culture from BFI Publishing, please write to:

BFI Film Classics
BFI Publishing
21 Stephen Street
London W1T 1LN